MARGINS

SYDNEY UNIVERSITY PRESS

The University of Sydney Master of Publishing Program, the
University of Sydney in association with the School of Letters, Art
and Media and SYDNEY UNIVERSITY PRESS
www.sup.usyd.edu.au

Sydney University Press

Fisher Library F03

University of Sydney NSW 2006 AUSTRALIA

Email: info@sup.usyd.edu.au

National Library of Australia Cataloguing-in-Publication entry

Title:	Margins : the Sydney University anthology 2009 / University of Sydney.
ISBN:	9781920899486 (pbk.)
Subjects:	Australian literature--21st century--Collections.
Other Authors/Contributors:	University of Sydney.
Dewey Number:	A820.8

CONTENTS

INTRODUCTION

Craig Silvey

My mother likes to tell me that I was born an old man.

To be fair, I did very little to disprove that. As a child I would often wake and waddle reluctantly out of bed, bleary-eyed after spending the night secretly reading under my covers by torchlight; I'd then slap the counter and demand my morning coffee (low caffeine, generously sugared) before fanning out the newspaper and clucking over current affairs.

I had a strong suspicion I was very different. But I knew enough about the fate of eccentric children not to appear that way. I didn't want to be one of those kids forced to the side by the rolling boulder of normalcy. I didn't want to be left behind or left alone.

So I learned to mimic my way out of displacement and recalibrate my behaviour to fit, always knowing that it felt like a counterfeit.

It was strange, having the ability to fit in everywhere, yet knowing that I didn't fit in anywhere at all. And in a lot of ways, I think those same socially nomadic principles I adopted as a child still persist, and they might have helped me become a better writer.

Because although I'm more comfortable living in the margins now, I don't ever want to lose that connection to the rolling ball.

I suspect it is where authors need to live: equally a part of the world, and apart from the world. The most important books connect the margins to the middle; they facilitate the conversation, and make us less alone, less suspicious, less fearful. Art is the best bridge between the two. And if you're going to engineer that, you've got to spread yourself as thin as you can, you've got to know both places.

Writing from the middle for the middle, or the margins for the margins has never held much interest for me. It doesn't promote real understanding, it doesn't cultivate the kind of broad conversation that really pushes things forward, that shifts thinking and challenges old ideas. Just as in biology, it's the adopted mutations that foster evolution and make us stronger and better humans; it's new ideas from the periphery, when introduced to the mainstream, that make a difference culturally.

And it's the characters who exist in the margins who hold the most allure for me, the ones I identify with the most. The ones who got left behind, who couldn't alter their behaviour, couldn't engage in the artifice or didn't want to. It's the observers that I love. The listeners. Because it's most often the quietest people who have the most to say. It's those most displaced who are worth following and distilling on the page, the characters who can't connect, can't communicate. As an author, you want to stitch the two. You want to give one a voice and make the other listen. You want to weave together common threads, just as much as you want to celebrate what is different and distinct.

That's why collections like these are so vital. They represent a new conversation, new blueprints, new answers to old questions, new characters and stories. Most importantly, they're new shouts from the margins; a new collection of connections.

Craig Silvey is the author of Rhubarb *(Fremantle Press) and* Jasper Jones *(Allen & Unwin), winner of the 2009 'Indie Book of the Year' Award 2009.*

A BEGINNER'S GUIDE TO WRITING

Zachary J Phillips

The darkness sat heavily in the air, the moon beaming down upon the world below. From the window, a solitary figure watched, breathing heavily with anticipation. There was only one option now, and that was to stand ground, just like the Spartans of old. He would fall, but it would be glorious. Suddenly, a gunshot echoed in the still night air. The man dropped to his knees just as the glass shattered, the bullet missing him by millimetres —

'A bullet?' a quizzical voice interrupted, breaking the concentration in the room.

'Yeah, what's wrong with a bullet?' replied the author with the voice of a man who had been woken from a particularly delightful dream.

'Well, I don't mean to sound rude or anything,' said the critic, 'but don't you think it's a little bit cliché?'

'How do you mean?'

'Everyone today uses bullets and guns. It's so barbaric. Every story you see, someone gets shot. It becomes a little bit predictable, and the last thing you want in your story is for the reader to know what's coming.'

'Ah, I see your point. Don't worry,' said the author, cracking his knuckles in preparation. 'I know exactly what to do here.'

Suddenly, a flash of light filled the night air. The man dropped to his knees just as the glass melted and a wave of heat passed above his head, the laser missing him by millimetres —

'Whoa, hang on there just a moment. Am I reading that correctly? A *laser*?'

'Yeah, what's wrong with a laser? It's new, it's futuristic and it gives the element of surprise to the story. I mean, no one would have guessed that there was going to be a laser attack!' The author was immediately transported to a world of robots and hi-tech machines, only to be brought back to reality by a nagging voice.

'But that's not the point! It doesn't fit in with the scenario and people won't be able to appreciate your, uh ... *creativity*. Besides,' he added matter-of-factly, 'if they had made lasers, surely they would have made laser-proof windows.' With a scoff the critic turned away to gaze thoughtfully at the window. 'Yes, definitely laser-proof windows.'

'Ah, another excellent point.'

An arrow whizzed through the open window. Archers had been a nuisance in this neighbourhood before, but never to this extent. Of late, they seemed to have multiplied like rabbits —
'YOU CAN'T USE A BOW AND ARROW!'

The author was stunned. 'Calm yourself, my friend. Remember the exercises. Breathe in — one, two, three — breathe out — one, two, three. Is that better? You know how I feel when you yell.'

'Sorry, and thanks. I don't know what came over me.' With a glance at the computer and what was written there, the critic suddenly remembered and grimaced, as if he had been struck in the gut by a medicine ball.

'Anyway,' said the author cheerfully, 'you were saying?'

'Ah, yes. You can't use a bow and arrow. It's nearly as obscure as a laser. I mean, who uses a bow and arrow to kill someone in modern suburbia?'

The author paused and thought, not realising that this was a rhetorical question. 'Maybe a French archer from the 1600s found a wormhole and was transported to the modern day, relying on nothing more than his bow and arrow and wit for survival.'

'Excuse me?' the critic said, only to realise it would have been much funnier to say *excusez-moi*.

'Yeah, French is great! Think about it.' The author was in awe, getting more and more excited as his train of thought took him further. 'A few people could understand him, but not all would. It's a division of cultures! Man ... This has the potential to be remembered right up there with *North and South*, as far as social commentary goes.'

The critic hit the writer on the head. 'That's so stupid.'

'Well,' said the author, annoyed, 'what do you suppose I do?'

There was a slight pause as the critic decided how to phrase himself. 'You could use a bullet.'

'A bullet?' The writer bit his lip to stop a string of curses.

'Yeah,' the critic said slowly and cautiously. 'It's traditional, people can relate to it. All in all, it's a win-win situation for writer and reader.' He looked pleased with himself, as if the gun scenario had been his idea all along.

'Hmm, I suppose you're right.'

The man dropped to his knees just as the glass shattered, the bullet missing him by millimetres. He swore loudly over the volley of bullets. When the deafening noise subsided, he peaked out of the window —

'It's "peeked", not "peaked".'

The author slowly turned. 'Did you just say the same word tw—'

'No!' the critic cut him off before he could get started. 'I said "peeked", not "peaked".'

There was a blank stare.

The critic clenched his jaw. 'Okay, you don't want peaked, like you have it. Replace the "ea" with a double "e".'

'Why?' he asked, his interest piqued.

'Because ... because it doesn't make sense like that.'

'But "peaked", the way I have it, is a word, right?"

'Yes, but it refers to quantity, height ... a mountain peak, the stock market peaked.'

'Ah, my mistake. Luckily, I have you here to guide me through the treacherous terrain of English. Ah, these homophones are confusing.'

'What?'

'A homophone. A word that sounds the same as another but is spelt differently. Like "peek" and "peak".'

'Just fix it.'

'Did you know it comes from Greek?'

'What on Earth are you talking about?'

'Homophone. It's made up of two Greek words. Well, two ancient Greek words. Homos, which means "same" or "common", and phōnē, which means "sound". So it means "same-sound".'He looked very pleased with himself, but the critic was in no mood for any of what the writer optimistically named 'fun facts'.

'Please, can we just get this done?'

When the deafening noise subsided, he peeked out of the window. There was no one to be seen. All he could see was the moon coming from behind a mountain peak.

The author looked very happy at his newfound mastery of the two words.

'Well, well, well,' a voice said from behind him. 'You thought you could steal my money and get away with it?'

'Money? Another cliché, my friend.'
'Oh, sorry.'

'You thought you could steal my child and get away with it?'

'Oh, that's better. Why did he steal the child though?'
'Ah, you'll find out, dear critic. Give it time.'

The man stood tall and spoke quietly. 'I did what was right.'

'Right? It was right to take my only child? The one thing

I have left to remind me of my wife, who died in a tragic boating accident off the coast of Cuba a year ago today in a devastating attack by drug lords? You're sick. You disgust me.'

'This baby —'

A laser was levelled at the first man's head.

'Hey!'

'Oh!' The author caught himself just in time. 'I'm sorry. But you're sure about the laser?'

'Yes! Get rid of it!'

'Fine, fine.'

A gun was levelled at the first man's head. 'Tell me, I need to know ... why did you kidnap my baby?'

The man sighed deeply. 'You see ... this child —'

'Excellent! You're building suspense!'

'This child is the cure to cancer!'

'And now you've ruined it.' The critic sighed and slumped back in his chair.

'How so?'

'A baby is the cure to cancer? Come on ...'

'Hey, I have poetic license here. It stays.'

The critic sighed again and started picking at his fingernails.

The President dropped his gun —

'Oh please ...'

— and stared in astonishment at his baby girl. 'My daughter is the cure to cancer?'

'I'm afraid so, sir. I have no choice but to take her away to conduct some experiments.'

The President stood in amazement. 'I can't let you do that,' he said, and quickly drew a pistol from his ankle holster and shot his foe in the forehead.

'No, wait ...' said the writer with a crazed smile, 'I suppose that's a little cliché, huh?'

The critic groaned. 'Just a tad, but I suppose it's a bit late now.'

The President levelled his pistol but, before he could fire, his adversary's face spontaneously combusted and he dropped to the floor.

'Hang on, you can't do that!'

'Why not?'

'It's impossible!'

'I'll have you know that there are several official records of spontaneous human combustion,' the author said pompously.

'I don't care! It's ridiculous! It doesn't fit!'

'Hang on,' said the writer. 'So you expect me to keep the reader entertained, guessing what's coming next —'

'Yes! But by keeping it within limits! It has to be logical!'

There was another pause. 'You want me to shock the reader by sticking to possibilities?' the author said slowly and deliberately.

'Uh ...' The critic hesitated.

'To logic?'

'Yes,' he answered, wincing.

'How on earth can you shock someone with realism?'

The President laughed at his easy victory, and then flew out of there in a blaze of glory to the White House, where he quickly stripped off his Superman outfit and entered the Conference Room.

THE END

'That was crap.'

'I quite like it,' said the writer with an air of contentment that is usually only seen in children under seven.

'But you broke all the rules! It was dribble! Incoherent! This was the worst thing I have ever critiqued! And I've read my teenage daughter's poetry!'

And in a rage the critic left, slamming the door behind him. The writer, pleased to have some solitude, looked at his piece and grimaced. He took a deep breath, and then held down the backspace key.

'Why would anyone want to write?' he asked himself.

ACCEPTANCE (WHEN THE SMELL OF DEATH GETS UP YOUR NOSE)

Ingrid Kesa

An organised departure from an organised life, on your birthday.
Thought through to the end.
Your birthday will be a monument to our wonderful loving memory of you.

1994
That was when my Opa turned into a ghost
I remember looking in front of me
I could not see. My vision, my recollection
Veiled by smoke

No flowers by request
He was never one for fuss, superfluous words
Breath wasted
An Aries, all in all

I am too young to remember the whole of those days
My Opa in his hospital bed (pale sheets, pale skin)
The funeral parlour (grey skies, grey skin)
Or the sad parties afterwards
The long faces and smudged eyes
No music was played

I was much younger then
I had to stand on a platform to reach the bathroom sink
To wash out my mouth, examine my skin
My memory has collected bits of those days
Gaps filled in
By looking at photographs, hearing stories, imagining

He came from Europe, decades before
To ink blueprints of impossible angles, shade monochrome
And escape war
He brought with him a guttural German spit
Wife and pipe
They set up house in Heidelberg, the name reminiscent of
home
They filled rooms with artefacts, treasures from around the
globe
Monaro glass blown into bubbles

Whittled wood fashioned into animal formations
Shelves heavy with literature

Years on they had a child
Just one, who they assigned the name of a saint (he came out with a halo of golden hair)
My father was once a baby — imagine that!
My Opa veiled by smoke
My Oma polishing, fixing, tidying
Always engaged

The first time I met my Opa (when consciousness kicks in)
I was scared
Then leapt into his outstretched arms
The invisible pull of ancestry
In the photograph, I am wearing a paper crown
And perched up on his shoulder, my hair touching the ground
A branch of his tree
He let his Spartan composure crack for the flash
Thin lips curled up, crows feet around eyes, proud of blood-ties
The smell of tobacco woven into the threads of his clothes
Burnt my nose

Cancer came, a week before he turned eighty
Poisoned his blood, blackened his lung
By this stage, I could read and write the basics
Even tie my own shoelaces

I could finger-paint and ride a trainer bike
It was not enough
I wish I were capable of dense conversation
Music, art, literature, history, philosophy
With my famous architect grandfather
He had so much to teach me
I inherited his taste for fine food, eye for aesthetic, and
Prominent Rembrandt nose

We drove down to Melbourne in early January
It was an ambitious journey
My new brother was restless the entire trip
Kicking at the air with blue booties
Gummy and swollen in the seat next to me
He demanded so much of my mother's time
I wanted her minutes all for myself — not fair.
The bald boy was getting in the way
Gnawing on her teat
Milking her love for all it was worth

It felt like days locked in that car
I guess it was

We arrived one morning or evening, I can't remember which
The interminable time when dusk is the same colour as day
A day before his birthday and not a minute too soon
My Oma was in the kitchen
Polishing, fixing, tidying, always engaged
My Opa was in the hospital, half-dying
Veiled by smoke

I remember the overwhelming smell of hospital linoleum
splashed with bleach
It burnt my nose
The ward was full of deflated people
Leathery and dusty flesh
Soon to melt to bones
My Opa's bed was near a window
On the table lay a virgin bible
A photograph of my brother and me (sent out with Christmas cards)
And a pipe

He was unresponsive, exhausted
His expression showed no sign of ache
Just Acceptance
I asked him, with innocence achievable only through infancy
What do you want for your birthday?
He took a while to reply but said
I want to die
Holding his hand in my own
I almost understood
For now
For the young girl who could read and write the basics
Even tie her own shoelaces ...
That was good enough

The next day, we bought him a cake
His lids were fastened
Skin blue

Lifeless
His face showed eighty years come to rest
The ravines and planes of his visage
Told tales of suffering, love, triumph
Acceptance
The cake melted in the midday sun
A pool of Harlequin colours
Mixed with the tears of my Oma

Lots of people who I did not know
Hugged me at the funeral
Most with glasses, hearing aids, walking sticks
Among other signs of age
Who said, it is very sad
I, however, knew
That my Opa's last birthday wish had come true
And for now, that was good enough

AEROPLANE

Catriona Daly

Bing! 'Crew, prepare cabin for take off.'

Bing! 'Please fasten seatbelts.'

Bit late for seatbelts isn't it? You don't go through life with a little red light flashing and binging at you before turbulence ... 'Please fasten seatbelts — goldfish dying, grandma sick and divorce approaching.'

A life jacket would have been nice.

Even half of that.

A life.

I could use a new coat.

I can't say I'm completely at ease sitting here, awaiting take off. It's not just the obese toad huffing and puffing all over more of my seat than his own, or the squeaky voiced enthusiast down the aisle. It's the plane. It smells. And smell is the closest sense to memory. It's somewhat ironic that it's an aeroplane ...

'Aeroplanes' was one of Brad's favourite games. We played it last Saturday — seems an age ago. Now I'm here in this stuffy plane, while he waits for me at a home to which I will never return. It was just me and him in our flat that Saturday, the sun not yet hidden, offering the glimmer of a dream-coated afternoon. Dusk I think they call it. We held each other close, arms entwined in an embrace beyond either of us, until I would extract him from my bosom, slowly, counting down from ten. Ten ... nine ... eight ... His face would swell with anticipation, lips creeping into a cheeky grin that gave me hope that everything might turn out okay. Five ... four ... he'd start giggling, a sound like a heart beating on its own for the first time after ten years of life support ... three ... two ... writhing in my hold ... one ... he began to fly, high above emotion. Whirring him around the room we would fly to Africa, Russia, France, the North Pole.

Then came the sweat, the exhaustion, and we collapsed into each other, fits of giggles and heavy panting. I would carefully lower his petite shape, cradling him in my arms, holding him slightly out from me until our noses were touching, his little legs dangling from my waist.

'I love you, mummy.'

Staring into those chocolate-coated eyes I saw his father. An intense hate of proportions previously unbeknown to me surged through my womb, stretching my skin hard and taught against my bruised form. All the hairs covering my body were pulled and knotted, physically entangling me in the web of pain I had been living in for years. I was furious and I was remembering. I was finally remembering. And that's where the red light should have started flashing, warning me, please fasten seatbelts. But it didn't, and the memories came flooding back like a river irresponsive to even the harshest constructs.

I saw him at our old house in Berowra. I was ten. He would sit in my favourite woven armchair, but I didn't mind. Sitting there, dressed in his senior school uniform, blue blazer, stripes, pleated pants — he was my friend. I see myself running towards him, arms outstretched, awaiting his familiar embrace. He used to let me sit on his lap all the time. For the first few years of my life I thought he was a fairytale. His last name was Prince, but concepts of identity had not yet been explained to me and so a Prince was a Prince, who got whatever he wanted.

He was a lot older than me, one of my older cousins, but he always played with me when he came over. He would tell me stories, stroking my back, my hair, my cheek, as I gazed into his mint eyes completely immersed in the worlds he created for me. My father left that year. Prince was there when he left. My mum was crying, screaming, but Prince just took me away, tucked me into my bed and kissed me like I'd seen Mummy and Daddy do before the yelling. 'Everything will be alright bubs, I'm here ...' I fell asleep with him half beside, half on top of me. I remember feeling safe. I stopped sleeping with a teddy bear after that night.

I saw him in the kitchen of Mum's apartment in Parramatta. I was fourteen. He was cooking something; Mum was working late again. I'd thrown my school bag on the floor and run, like a child once more, into his arms. The kids at school hadn't believed me when I'd told them I had a Prince for a boyfriend. They'd told the teacher and she'd organised this big interview thing with my Mum. The more I talked, the more mum cried until she got so angry that she started yelling at me, telling me I was a dirty rotten liar. I stopped telling people about Prince after that. It was our little secret.

I saw him lying on my bed, in Mum's second apartment in Glebe. I was sixteen. He was unbuttoning my blouse, shuddering at the cross embroidered on the left breast pocket. He was kissing me, leaning, heaving on top of me — Mum was working late again. I told him about this boy I liked. I honestly thought he'd want to know. But he got angry. He started yelling, told me I was a traitor, a whore ... I started crying and the tears seemed to make him angrier until he lashed out and struck my cheek. I was scared, I could feel the red of my skin rising. He started to kiss it better, I relaxed in his hold ... but then his kissing got angrier and angrier until he was holding my arms above my head and I was screaming for him to stop but he wouldn't listen. He pushed harder and harder, consuming every inch of me until I just focused on the aeroplane shaped crack on my ceiling, half-believing that by making an inanimate object animate, the animate might become a little less real.

I saw him in my son. Every day. Grinning up at me. I saw myself smashing Brad's little head against the wall, again and again, each resonating thud giving me a thrilling sense of liberation. As his limp body sprung to life under my merciless grip, I squeezed every ounce of his father out of him, and left him waiting in our empty flat.

Bing! 'Crew, prepare cabin for landing.'

Bing! 'Please fasten seatbelts.'

Tears started to slide down my cheek, pooling on the hurt he had left with his hand. Clutching the worn seatbelt that had probably never saved a life in its entire existence, I hoped that this could be its first.

ALL QUIET ON THE BACKYARD FRONT

Kat de Jong

Did you know that Zyklon B, the deadly hydrogen cyanide concoction used in the exterminations at Auschwitz-Birkenau concentration camp, was originally manufactured as a simple insecticide? And that Bayer, one of the founders of the IG Farben conglomerate that held the patent for Zyklon B, is currently one of the largest producers of pesticides and insecticides, turning over a 32.4 billion euro profit in the year 2007? I find myself thinking about these rather sinister relationships today, of all days, because today is the day that I dread most every year. Today is pest control day.

I have diplomatic relations with insects, as I believe them to be the original modernists due to their desire to discover the unknown natural world and to understand mankind. Therefore, I am perfectly content for my limbs and digits to serve as meeting places, bathhouses and pit stops for these insect ambassadors, such as the *Musca domestica* (common house fly). As strange as it sounds, I even find myself becoming offended when insects take one quick tour of my epidermis only to immediately fly off. I am worried that I've become an unfashionable landing strip in the eyes of these insect philosophes.

However, it must be said that I have a slightly less than diplomatic relationship with arachnids. For years, we fought a stalemate, wherein their ambassadors, mainly *Badumna insignis* (black house spider) would come within my lands and I would swiftly order their executions. Finally, an armistice was called and a peace pact was subsequently drawn up. In exchange for me not killing arachnids and their allies, they do not send their extermination squad, the *Atrax robustus* (funnel-web spider) or the *Latrodectus hasseltii* (red-back spider) after me. Unfortunately, despite the proven success of this treaty of neutrality and my best efforts to change their stance, my parents are less in favour of appeasement and more in favour of wars of attrition.

I have given speeches filled with so much pathos, ethos and logos that would amaze Aristotle himself. I have pointed out both the financial and fiscal costs of wars of attrition; it cost Germany 226 billion Reichsmark in 1919. I have presented informative yet humorous lectures about how vital the symbiotic mutualism is between insects, arachnids and sustainable backyard ecology. I have even sermonised about how pest control actively contravenes the Christian Sixth Commandment of 'Thou Shalt Not Kill', but to no avail. The Allied Forces of Parents continue to fight them on the landing grounds, in the fields and in the streets and in the hills. They refuse, conditionally or unconditionally, to surrender. So committed to victory are my parents that on those rare occasions where The Axis Power of Creepy Crawlies momentarily appear to be winning the war for supremacy, they are willing to bring out the insect equivalent of the Atomic Bomb, namely the 'Pest Control Guy'. Therefore, I am left with only one solution. Exodus.

As soon as D-Day (Dreaded-Day) is announced, I commence a relocation program, capturing as many insects and arachnids as possible and releasing them to safety. Initially, I took the time to investigate where the choicest and most scenic places for both insects and arachnids could migrate, including the nearby bush reserve filled with a smorgasbord of food and shelter, the across-the-street-neighbour's beautiful landscaped garden complete with a resort style pool, the front yard of my next door neighbour's place that can best be described as providing luxury desert safari-style adventure. However, as the date looms closer, I no longer care about these trivial, insignificant details and I relocate my soon-to-be refugees anywhere; anywhere at all where the toxic gas won't reach them and they'll be safe from harm.

However, when the bomb itself is finally dropped, I realise just how futile was my exercise in exodus. Whilst some bravely hold out a strong resistance, such as the *Eriophora transmarina* (garden orb weaving spider) bravely spinning a web next to the clothes line, most succumb immediately to the toxins. I can only watch helplessly as *Periplaneta australasiae* (Australian cockroaches) crawl out from beneath rocks, and from under fridges only to perform death throes on the red brick pavers. *Camponotus consobrinus* (banded sugar ants) leave behind whole colonies, eerily similar to those evacuated villages in provincial wartime France. The carnage is terrible and by the time of the Last Post, the war is over and victory is complete. It is all quiet on the backyard front, the killing field littered with the carcasses of the fallen.

As I return to the clothes line, I discover the body of the brave resistance spider whom I espied earlier. Whilst its two-part body is now unnaturally curled inward like a ball, its eight delicate legs are still wrapped around its web. It is evident that the spider held out for as long as possible. Gently, with the web attached like a paratrooper in his 'chute, I remove it from the clothes line and bury it in the nearby garden bed, with a piece of pine bark serving as a crude grave-marker — *Eriophora transmarina*. Killed In Action, 5 December 2008.

Next year, I think I'll start the exodus earlier.

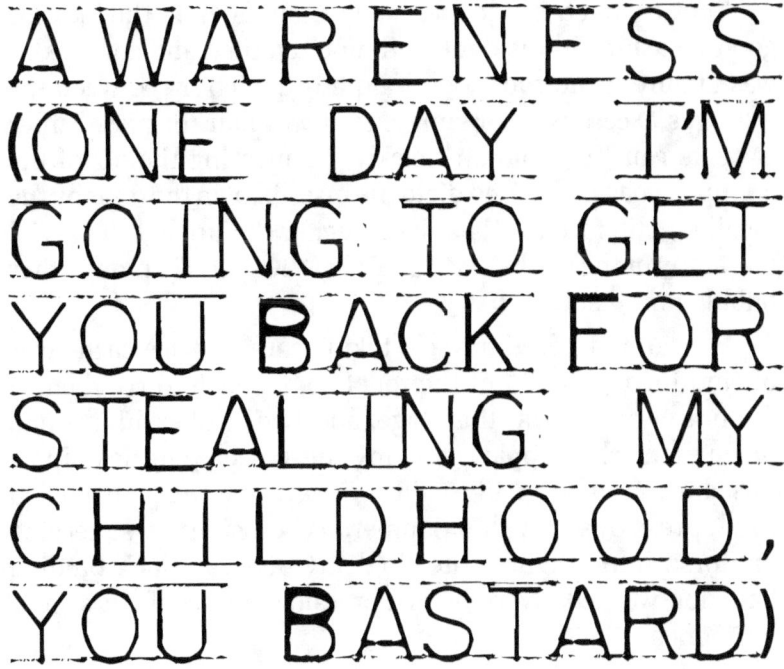

AWARENESS (ONE DAY I'M GOING TO GET YOU BACK FOR STEALING MY CHILDHOOD, YOU BASTARD)

Ingrid Kesa

The first time I got my period, I was at the local swimming pool with my brothers. It was my twelfth birthday. I was in the toilet block, getting changed into my swimsuit: a once-bright thing, colours blunted from chlorine, elastic loosened from wear. My feet slipped across the slimy concrete with each step. An imposing black woman was peeling off her clothes in front of me, her nipples as large as saucers and as pink as the inners of her eyes. She looked fierce, athletic, the kind of lap-swimmer I annoyed by throwing my delicate body into her lane during some game or another, interrupting her strokes.

I got changed inside a toilet cubical, latching the lock for good measure. It was dank and mouldy, tiled and confined. I wasn't sure if the cool pool of liquid squelching between my toes was excess water wrung out of wet hair, or piss. Either way, its caustic odour was sickly, permeating the air of the cramped space. I noticed dialogue inscribed on the door by the illegible, illiterate hands of local teens who upheld the social hierarchy of the pool — TRACEY YA DOG SLUT! among other bubble font insults.

I began to undress myself, taking care to place each layer of clothing on the lid of the toilet so as not to dirty them. I did not wear a bra at this stage, and two swollen lumps had made themselves apparent on my chest, each pinprick nipple raised toward heaven like a flower ready to unfurl. I had tried to suppress this growth on numerous occasions by squeezing my torso into a tight white singlet. Of course, such binding had not worked over the irrepressible force of persistent hormones.

A flimsy pallid skin stretched over the ribs below those confusing protuberances, and, further down, chalk-soft hip bones jutted out in awkward symmetry. A dozen crude, arcane hairs had pushed their way through the tender follicles of the V between my legs; those same unwished for hairs had sprouted out from the shallow gorges of my armpits in cruel curls and uneven lengths.

I peeled my cotton underwear off, pastel-coloured with rosebud and lace, the kind that is only worn by young girls and old women. I placed the panties on top of the pile of material I had shed and noticed a red smear staining the baby yellow. I first associated the cherry-red pigment with a nosebleed, but the concealed folds of skin between my legs shuddered slightly when met with my unacquainted touch, and my fingers emerged sticky with warm blood.

Heather was proudly the only girl in grade five who had her rags. She was also the only girl who wore a bra — a gaudy, obvious padded thing her mother had bought her, like the equivalent of clip-on earrings. Unfortunately, mostly for the mother's nymphet ambition, her tits hadn't plumped at all, chest still flat and sexless, her silhouette still the linear shadow of preteen androgyny.

The Sisters at school had talked about menstruation in hushed voices with guilty mannerisms, persistently looking over their shoulders in case He had heard. The Headmaster's office was right next door and he did not like to be disturbed. They had spoken of pads and tampons, the latter of which they discouraged. They had not, however, given any direct answers as to where such items could be acquired. I think I half expected the visage of Mary Magdalene to appear, a lucent hand extended, overflowing with a holy offering of rhinestone-studded sanitary napkins. No such glowing apparition appeared to save me and instead I had to make do with crude makeshift methods.

I stopped the crimson invasion from running down my thighs by shoving a wad of abrasive toilet paper up into that delicate curve to which I'd never before endeavoured to introduce my raw touch. I pulled my swimsuit on, the material saggy and shapeless around all the crucial areas.

My brothers were waiting for me outside the change rooms, their bare-chested bodies interlocked in a primal display of masculinity.

'We thought you'd died in there,' came one of their voices from deep inside a headlock.

'Sorry,' I said, feeling self-conscious, shifting my position so as to accommodate the prickly toilet paper, hoping against hope that they wouldn't notice any signs of womb walls replenishing. Apparently they hadn't, and naturally expected me to chase after them as they ran up the CAUTION WET SURFACE ramp to the pool, oblivious to the initiation into womanhood I was undergoing.

I sat on the edge of the pool, dangling my legs into its azure abyss. I noticed an old man, my father's age if not older, looking at me from out of the corner of his eye. He had skin like hide, made tough by the sun. He continued to look at me as though I was a piece of fruit he was considering plucking from a tree. Almost suddenly, my exposed shoulders felt different, vulnerable, and my hair blowing in the wind whispered secrets in my ear, secrets I did not want to hear.

They told tales of fertile lands inside of me, rolling hills plush with the essence of life, fruitful flesh-speckled crops after dry summers, rivers flowing with productivity, wild tides lapping against the banks, pink anatomy peeled wide open, tenderness about to burst like bubblegum, contracting muscles, curves of pleasure and pain dusted in slivers of silver-blonde hair, the excitement of Christmas morning, lights around the tree like a necklace, feverishly unwrapping layers of skin, spongy softness inside.

I watched from the corner of my eye as he furiously rubbed the front of his red Speedos. His eyes were full of what I thought was anger and I could not help but feel sorry for him. There were more beautiful females at the pool than me, more juicy red apples with a white flesh inside. Women lounged about on deckchairs in bikinis, sunning themselves in the midday rays, conscious of being watched, their body parts arranged deliberately so as to agree with the pull of gravity. Groups of gregarious teenage girls sat in spas, baby-faces bobbing in the bubbles, gossiping and giggling, an onslaught of oestrogen. Mothers plump with happiness played with newborns in the paddling pool, breasts still to shrink to original size. Yet his gaze did not waver.

As the man's rubbing culminated into a blur of hands (big hands, big hairy hands, the left wrist with a watch), time froze, and in those few seconds I saw my childhood slip away ...

... sitting on dads shoulders so I could see the soccer goals more clearly mum kissing me on the cheek her lips softer than mohair school excursions to the aquarium wheels on the bus go round and round front seat is for nerds backseat is for squids cubby houses under the dining table complete with sheets for walls stuffed animals having feelings too the last day of term staying out til nightfall mum being worried hugging instead of yelling bike riding with my brothers lollipops after the doctors are we there yet grandma being the oldest person alive Easter Bunny Santa Claus tooth fairy fireflies trapped in glass jars the reassuring glow of light when darkness falls ...

... All that was lost forever, faded to memories like pale photographs where everything was better back in the 'old days'.

I can't remember any of the presents that I got for my birthday that year. All I know is that right there and then, sitting with my thin arms shielding my shoulders, water submerging my legs up to my knobbly knees grazed pink (it was against school rules to run in the open breezeway), a wad of soggy paper up my vagina and tears obscuring my vision, I knew that none of those things would make me feel the same as they always had. None of those things would be enough for me to know that everything would be okay now that I was twelve and had my period.

BONNIE

Melinda Mills

Bonnie is eight years old and she sits quietly on the sand. Her back presents to the shore, so she can keep a wary eye on the waves that relentlessly creep towards her. She works tirelessly on the engineering marvel created from sand, spade and bucket.

She turns her head to wave cheerfully, beckoning me to join her. Under her straw hat, her pink cheek is sprinkled with white grains of sand and her honey-coloured hair has turned dark from both sweat and sea.

She takes me on a tour of her sandcastle and moat. To me it looks like a blob of wet, soggy sand, but through Bonnie's eyes, I can see her fairytale creation.

'Take me swimming, mummy,' she asks gently.

There is nothing harsh or unkind about Bonnie. I have always described her as my pink, soft girl, and that is what she is. She doesn't ride a bike or throw a ball, would rather pretend to be a mermaid than swim her strokes and has an endearing habit of singing for pure joy, for no reason other than her own happiness. She is winsome and dreamy, unfocused and innocent, lovable by her very nature. She will always be naive. The world will not harden her or coerce her temperament into anything other than what she is. She is beautiful. She is unspoilt. She is uniquely quirky. Bright when she chooses and infuriatingly stubborn. She is her own mistress.

The rhythmic waves draw us hand in hand, up to her waist and my hips. I am short and she will be tall. She clings to my hand in the tidal salt.

'Don't let me go, mummy,' she begs.

I draw her further out into the waves and she clutches my hand. Finally, the water is too deep for her to stand nd she throws her arms possessively around my neck. We drift there in the rise and fall of the waves, with the sun sparkling through the water. We do not speak and there is an enfolding calm around us. We are our own world.

We float towards the shore and I carry her out of the waves. We trudge out of the foam and onto the beach. The hot sand burns our feet and we find the oasis of our towels. I lie on my stomach, so I can see Bonnie. She takes out her bucket and spade and proceeds to dig holes in the sand. She is cocooned in her imagination and hums a sweet, melodic tune. She smiles at me, as she flicks sand unknowingly across my towel. Crossly, I tell her to be more careful. She turns up her nose with a snooty 'humph' and turns her back on me, continuing to dig persistently. It amazes me how she can be absorbed in such an inane task, but I guess that is the nature of children.

She rolls off her towel onto the sun-heated sand, oblivious of the sand that sticks to her heat-flushed skin. The sun has somehow managed to find her upturned nose and it is sunburnt. Her cheeks are rosy from digging, or the sun, but probably both. It is time to shower off and leave the beach. Bonnie shoves all her beach toys into her clear plastic backpack and races to the outdoor shower with a squeal of delight.

BRIO

Amelia Dale

Mr James Church did not like the new company building. He wasn't sure why; it was larger, newer, closer to his home, closer to the city. It even had something of a view. But every time he crossed its threshold to his office, he felt as if black liquid was seeping into his chest and mind. Perhaps it was the smell.

'Most definitely,' said Francis, James' colleague, unpacking a variety of framed photographs and arranging them elegantly on his own desk. 'This tower used to be used by a media relations company; naturally the air is still thick with odours foul.'

James nodded his buzzing head.

'That's enough unpacking and work for today,' proclaimed Francis, rubbing his thin hands together. 'It's almost ten. Let's see if the coffee machine has been set up yet.'

They meandered past men and women bent over boxes and Blu Tack. A woman in a beige pencil skirt was kneeling on the floor, plugging in the photocopier.

'Good morrow, Carol,' said Francis.

Carol stood up, looked at James, and a peculiar thing happened. James knew what Carol looked like (blue eyes, pancake make-up and a pinched looking face). He also knew that Carol was standing right in front of him. But Carol looked very different today. She had a painted clown face and a sardonic leer.

'Should we fetch you some coffee?' asked Francis.

'No thanks, I've had four cups already,' said the clown, and though it was speaking Carol's words, it said them in a voice that reverberated from beneath the building's dusty floor.

James did not hang around to hear Francis' reply; he ran to the bathroom and took several deep breaths. What had he done to deserve such a hallucination? He had gone to bed at a decent hour last night. And he was not mad; he was sure he was not mad. He ambled to the bathroom mirror, rubbing his thinning hair back from his forehead. He didn't look well at all. He hadn't even shaved this morning. Why hadn't Francis told him — hang on, that wasn't his face. It was hairy and disconcertingly feminine. He stared at it and a pair of stranger's eyes stared back at him. The bearded woman squashed her face up against the glass, flattening her nose and stretching her hairy cheek. James backed away into a cubicle. He locked the door, then unlocked it, looked up. No, she was still behind the mirror. Her bristly face split into an inaudible scream.

Francis sauntered into the bathroom. 'James, you okay? You looked pale and ran away ...'

James smiled weakly at Francis and gestured towards the mirror. 'I don't suppose you can see him — her — it?'

Francis frowned at the mirror. 'I can see you and me.'

'I must be going mad, then. Oh, what a nuisance,' groaned James, wiping his sweaty forehead with a hanky. 'You see —'

'No, I can't see. What's it you see?'

'A manly woman or a womanly man, beating at the glass with a white hairy fist, screaming and stuff.'

The thing in the mirror pulled out paper and a pen, hurriedly wrote something, then waved the paper at James. The handwriting was poor, and the letters had been flipped. Yet, by turning his head to one side and concentrating, James could read it. '"Beware Brio." What the hell does that mean? Why was Carol a clown?'

Francis shook his head. 'These things are beyond my comprehension.'

'I don't like this place,' muttered James. He touched his head with his fingers. Something was polluting it.

'You're home early,' said Mrs Church, James' wife. They had been married for nineteen years this spring. She worked, but never on Mondays. 'Sam will be pleased.'

Sam was their son.

'I wasn't — don't feel well,' said James.

'Poor dear. I hope it's not the flu. I think it's going around. I'll pick Sam up from school then. He didn't want to go to school this morning,' she said, beginning to sweep the living room. 'I think he's being bullied. Do you feel very bad?'

'Oh no,' said James. 'I'm sure I'll be well tomorrow.'

While Mrs Church was driving Sam home from school, the phone rang.

It was Francis.

'You feeling better now?'

'Yes,' said James, while shaking his head at the same time.

'Well, you won't be when I'm done with you. Beware Brio, was that the words? I did some research, in work hours of course, and Brio was the name of a clown. In 1961, the Squiddlebug Circus arrived in Sydney. The clown act involved Brio shooting his fellow clown, Panache, with a water pistol. Except, on one particular performance, he used a loaded semiautomatic. Brio gunned down Panache, every one of his circus colleagues on stage and a vast number of audience members. He then shot himself. I thought this stuff only happened in American schools. Ah, here's a photo of Brio. When you saw a clown, was there black around the eyes, blue on the mouth and a purple nose?'

James swore in assent, but he lacked the strength to say much more.

'I knew it!' cried Francis. 'The company's new building is on the very ground where this massacre took place.'

There was the sound of the garage door opening. His wife and son were home. James held the phone limply between his dripping palms.

Francis continued talking. 'When you first started seeing things I thought Carol had slipped you some LSD or you were going schizo, but now I've read this, all I can think is that you see dead people like that creepy child ...'

The door slammed shut. Sam and Mrs Church walked through the hallway, looking like shadows from a life now lost. James waved at them and carried the cordless phone upstairs.

'But I don't want to see dead people,' he hissed, as soon as his family was out of earshot. 'What's the point of people being dead if they keep on popping up all over the place?'

'That's a very conventional attitude to take, James. They don't just appear for anyone, you know. You're special.'

'No,' groaned James. 'Special is a word the teachers call my son when they want to give him extra maths coaching. I'm quite content to be ordinary. I — I know you find work boring and pine for bigger and better things, but I don't. I'm fine being not special. Why did Brio appear to me, Francis? Why is it that I have to beware him?'

'Perhaps there is something in you he likes, Mr Shaver.

Yes, your shipment will be arriving as soon as the truck crosses the border.' Francis hung up; James guessed the boss had just stepped into Francis' cubicle.

Sam was a bit quieter than usual during dinner, but spaghetti was his favourite, so perhaps he was just focusing on eating.

That night, James dreamt he was swinging on a trapeze in a ridiculous brown and orange leotard. He flew back and forth, the audience's faces blurred into an expression of rapture. The contortionist scratched her ear with her toe. The fire-eater ate. The tightrope-walker stood on the shoulders of the bearded lady who stood on the shoulders of the strong man. The clowns were in the corner and Brio had his gun.

Brio held the gun above his head, an expression of weird animal glee pasted on his painted face. James floated above the horrors, he thought he was invisible, but Brio met James's eyes. He gave James a goofy clown wave, while simultaneously blasting a bawling innocent. Brio looked at James with James's face.

'A bad dream?' asked Mrs Church.

'Yes,' said James. 'Did I wake you up?'

'Yes, when you screamed and tried to strangle me.'

'Did I — oh — oh I'm so sorry.'

'I know you didn't mean to,' said Mrs Church, 'but I'm rather frightened you'll do it again, so I think I'll go and sleep on the couch downstairs.'

'No — please don't leave me,' cried James, frightened of the night like a child. 'I won't go to sleep. I'll read this book and drink lots of water. Please stay and hold my hand.'

'What was your nightmare about?' asked Mrs Church.

'I see dead people,' said James.

'Well, if they're dead, strangling them won't do any good.'

'True,' said James. 'And the worst they can do is kill me, or drive me mad. I know I'll die eventually, but I won't let them make me mad.'

'That's fine,' murmured Mrs Church, dropping off to sleep.

'I love you, you know,' said James.

At work the next day, James looked at Carol and saw the clown face, but this time he managed to behave with irreproachable politeness towards Carol. James encountered the bearded lady in the bathroom mirror, this time he gave her a timid smile. Brio himself appeared in the work cafeteria, but James ignored the clown. Psychopathic clowns do not even deserve common courtesy.

James found that these horrors weren't horrors at all when you accepted them as merely annoying things to be borne, along with the rest of existence. James' boss, James' son's social maladjustment and Francis' excessive use of perfume were phenomena at least equally trying. It was true that James continued to see dead people and be haunted by Brio for the rest of his life, but he paid them less and less attention, and the passing of time made the supernatural seem nearly natural. It was true James still was troubled by nightmares, but it's a sad fact that most people are. And James learnt that he did not strangle his wife in his sleep when he wore a straitjacket to bed.

CENTRIFUGE

Pristine Ong

Kaleidoscope.

Place your hand on the seat beside you. There. It's still warm. The roller-coaster jerks to a stop and the jolt travels up your fingers. Here are the day's smells: sweat from your armpits, the ripeness of your hair, milkshake in the sun. Here are the people: the mother with bawling children, father with his phone, teenagers who loved the thrill. Here's the seatbelt wrapped around your stomach: tight, intimate; like a corset. It saved you from the plunge.

What a plunge.

Tick-tick-tick. The alarm clock goes off. I reach out for the button and almost fall off the bed. It's a steep drop. If I fall, what will catch me? The cold, tiled floor and the clothes from last night? There's the silk blouse, so soft as it came off. There are the black trousers, rough and prickly. I pull myself back up. Here he is, asleep, with the flutter of his eyelids as he dreams.

What time is it?

Still early.

What time is it?

Dusk.

He pulls me closer, wrapping his arms around me. I smell his perspiration. I close my eyes and enter his world — the constant ticking of the clock, the rhythmic push and pull of his body. No road, no sign, no boundary. I lose myself.

Swirling. The roller-coaster swerves inwards. These are your paths: the centrifuge or the straight drop. Here's a hand: it presses its palms into the air, stretching out its fingers to slide into a circle, reaching towards the centre, searching for the hand of another. Here, at the turning point, is the drop: it's a straight path that branches from the twist. If you fall, what will catch you but the parched grass and overstretched plastic tents beneath? Pull yourself in. Here, the safety of the corset.

Click.

Place your hand on the seat beside you. There's nothing. You're at the peak, ready to plummet down. What will keep you in? The corset loosens as your body slides backwards. Where's the hand at your side? You can't turn back. Here, your heart against the roller-coaster's rhythmic pound.

Peeling an apple. The red skin comes off like silk. Rawness beneath. It's a steep drop and the skin falls down, catching the twirl of the air. It collects on the tile, between my bare feet and his shoes.

Are you going?

It's time.

Where are you going?

Moving on.

He pulls me in, pressing his arms into me. My arms at my side, the steel blade at my thigh, pointing downwards like a compass. Perspiration beneath his shirt. No road or sign. Between us, the apple-red skin. In my hand, the apple: raw, fresh.

Place your hand on the seat beside you. Here. It's cool. You're at the point of centrifuge. Around you, seats are filling up, working inwards: fathers, mothers, children. The corset clips on and the noises collide: excitement, trepidation, impatience. It all clicks.

Kaleidoscope.

C I T Y
SOFTENED

Ben Daroczy

To flow

The city softly sounds

So aching

Through my every pore

And with

The rising of the red

City sunrise

Drives it more

And more for them

Is more for me

The silken sheet

Of fog on street

Like ants they come

And vultures leave

The looming flocks

To romance spots
The quiet crimes
Of docks
The splinter stick
Still stuck in lock
And still they mock
My drunken friends
The reprimand:
Means to an end

ETIQUETTE

Diana Quan

Oh! How

Marvellous to see you, you must

Drop by more often. How have

You been? No, nothing's wrong.

Whatever do you mean? Tea or

Coffee? Not much to eat, but

I'll fix you something.

Are you all right?

Why should you

Be asking me that? I'm fine.

You're hurting me. Let go.

Stop this? And do what?

You're moving away. Whatever for?

Come! Reach inside! Your hand goes right
Through, fascinating isn't it?
Come! Take my head! Drop it and break it
And see underneath white, faceless bone;
Tar and pitch, surging beneath noxious fumes.
Rather awful, I was going to get something done about
That, but, well, what will you recommend?

Talk to someone? And say what?

I'm talking to you now, aren't I
But I wonder, are you listening?
(Foul, fetid weakness; pathetic, sodden wretch!)
Excuse me, terribly sorry. I suppose it
Hardly matters, haha! Gaudy words
Drop from lips that close around thorns;
Pretty baubles tossed to bears —
Who's up for a bit o' bear-baiting!
Hysteria beneath a jester's hat
(No wonder you wish to leave)

Leave? And go where?

This place — just like any other,
Really. What use is scenery or
A change of space if one is barely
Here? Don't worry yourself!
I'm there. More crumpet? Spread
On the butter thick, watch the light
On the metal
Distort
And split
In an oily, oily rainbow
Spreading out.

Do you think this is that rare?

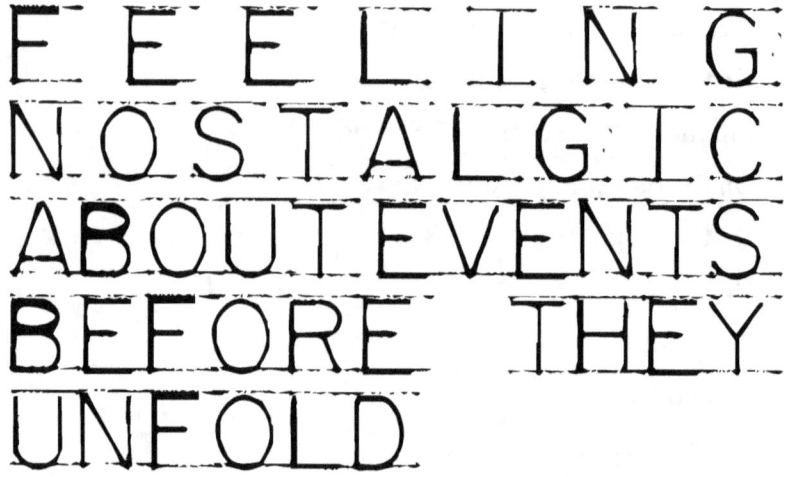

FEELING NOSTALGIC ABOUT EVENTS BEFORE THEY UNFOLD

Ingrid Kesa

The other night my mum drank too much wine, so she put on all these old records and started dancing this slow, clumsy dance. She reminded me of a beautiful ballerina with all the life sucked out of her veins. Watching her was like watching a moving collage of human emotion. It was for the ephemeral duration of that song that I felt closer to her than I ever have before. I saw every moment that had passed and every moment that was to follow, for me and for her. Our whole experience fused for the profound four minutes of that song's gauzy string pick-up and splintered melody.

There she was, age nine, with eyes the colour of fresh blue

toilet water and at least two big handfuls of freckles flung across her face from the left ear to the right, across the nose and dripping down the upper lip. I saw her meeting my dad for the first time — 'love' was not a dirty word back then. I imagined her leaving home, her parents standing on the front porch, half worried and half understanding, as she got onto the back of my dad's motorbike, her golden hair leaving behind a trail as the wind blew through it. I could see her burning her bra in her university days, taking off the corset of oppression and letting her armpit hair grow out in thick black tufts. Pregnant with me, at the front of a Led Zeppelin concert, being 'this' close to Robert Plant as he all but exploded out of his jeans that were so tight they could virtually stand up by themselves. At least that's how I imagine it to have been.

She told me that this one song reminded her of being my age. She'd go over to her friend's house with my dad and they'd play this same record and they'd dance around — the same dance but overflowing with the vim and vigour of vitality and the prospect of infinite horizons and endless languid Sunday afternoons and the unbreakable promise of the unfading perpetuality of fanatical love. One of her friends wore pottery bangles up to her elbows and would play the tambourine section by moving her arms about in the air.

It was a wistful moment between my mum and I — like staring into a really green ocean on a really grey day with someone that you love and who loves you back and you can feel them touch you before it actually happens and then they do touch you and you feel it but about one hundred times softer than how you thought that it would feel and you smile privately to yourself. It was a bit like that.

Tomorrow is my eighteenth birthday and I really wish it wasn't. I know I'm not meant to be so sad right now, but I can't help but feel an overwhelming sense of sympathy for my parents. I'm trying to imagine how they must feel at this very moment. My birthday is a most obvious, unwanted reminder of their own mortality and the way in which they've forgotten to notice the sun setting because of afternoon rush-hour traffic, how Sunday afternoons are synonymous with paperwork, how love has its limits after all these years. It scares me, because one day I'm going to be the one with the daughter turning eighteen tomorrow, lying in bed, nestled in the unapologetic curves of the familiar geography of an antique lover, thinking about these old songs that used to be happy at the time but are now sad because that time is gone forever.

FRAPPUCCINO

Matthew Ji Xing Cai

He quenches me down
with every gallon of skin and cells
over a frappuccino
that is essentially me.
I'm the ice in the blender
crackling noisily, disobediently
head-butting the see through glass.

It's very possible that I'm the chocolate
musk left greedily on his rough shaven top lip,
the naivety attached to his countenance.

He tells me, that within a few days
or years or however long it takes me
to read a worthwhile novel,

I will think he does me good.
And for the many moments while I wander
with him in this harsh brambled terrain

in which we collectively call
the city, I'm convinced.

Maybe my thoughts are like fermented milk,
fluid and susceptible to manipulative colourings;
wherein the flavour changes so much that I don't
even notice the calcium and proteins
in my initial tasteless taste.

And at the closing of this coffee break
I seem liquidated, and he refreshed in grasping
the many clashing ingredients of a frappuccino.
Still I'm undecided of what's preferable:

to either identify myself as a farce
of my former glory
in all of its chain stall logos
('vulgarising coffee' as the Venetians
would call it) left behind
on an alfresco tabletop

or an empty mass-produced plastic cup
sweating of unwanted residue
and readily to be disposed of
at the nearest bin.

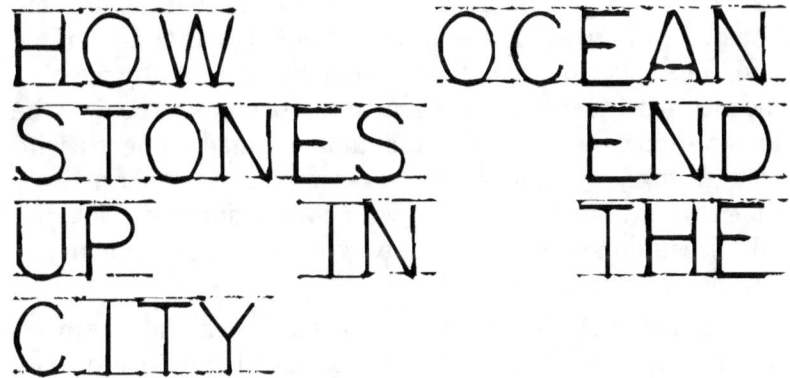

HOW OCEAN STONES END UP IN THE CITY

Karina Barker

I was kicking a stone down the street. One of those ones that'd been shaped by the ocean, but had somehow made its way to the city. I was thinking about this, how it got to the city, when I looked up and saw it — you — built out of nothing, wearing the facsimile of an expression I once saw for real.

***

It's a sad story this. It starts with a pair of trousers. Black, flat front, brushing the top of leather soles; they caught my eye in a whitewash of beige pleats. The crowd afforded me minutes to indulge in my attraction and I studied the lines of your face, the brown of your eyes, the lines of muscle that flank your spine and nuzzled the inside of your shirt. I tried to imagine the life that went with you and suddenly there I was, walking through your hypothetical front door, wrapping my hand around the back of your neck. Honey, I said, hello.

The crowd ebbed towards the conference room, but I stayed back and hung on the edges. There was a clipboard of papers handed to me and an offer to take my coat. Thank you, I said, no I'm okay. The doors were closing either side of me and there was a hand on the small of my back, gently pushing me forward. I turned around and it was, of course, you with the flat-fronted trousers. And in that moment made concrete with your gesture, my smile, four steps in sync, I knew instinctively that I would laugh alongside you: conspirators of a joke no one else understands. For I knew I got you, even before I knew a thing about you at all.

We met in the lobby after the launch; we hadn't arranged it but I knew you'd be there. And you asked me: So, are you a geek or a yuppie?

A journalist, I said. I'll be writing about the product. Yuppie?

Sales director. I'll be selling it to the shops for the geeky and yuppie.

I laughed, and it was like thunder cracking above the crowd. People turned and I covered my mouth with my hand. You grasped my wrist with ownership. Don't waste that, you said, and as you took your hand away I noticed the wedding band on your finger.

Later, standing at the hotel bar, you told me your wife was seven months pregnant.

That's wonderful, I lied. You nodded.

I asked about names and you told me you didn't really mind, it was up to her, it was her thing, really, anyway.

We talked about life, what we'd done until then, what we wanted to do from that point on, and all the things we'd done so differently. You seemed amazed enough at the things I was saying to make me blush like I was eight years old.

My wife, you said, she's content with so little.

Oh, I thought, but you're so much.

Our stories were tripping over each other, and I felt safe and scared at once. You were laughing and I took off my coat and we were seated in a booth at the back of the bar.

You said: I'm so glad I met you.

I said nothing. Then: I'm hungry. Should we ask for some nuts?

Actually, I should go, you said. I should be getting home, you said. It's late, you said. I have to go, you said. You handed me your card. I gave you mine. Can I get you a cab? Will you be okay?

I'll be fine. Take care.

As I shrugged my coat back on, I was numb. And yet it felt like the first time I had ever really felt at all.

Every day you could've called, and every day you didn't. The silence was screeching. I fingered your card. Sniffed it, even. It smelt like cardboard, and I wondered why I cared so much.

Then, a Tuesday. My computer screen wobbled, *beep beep*: a message. Can I call you some time?

Of course, I wrote, after no thought at all. And fifteen seconds later you did.

I tumbled down the stairs with my phone in my hand. At the bottom, out of breath but in private, I said: Hello?

It's me, you said, in an 'only me' sort of way. Which threw me a little.

How are you? I said.

Good ... good. And then just like that you said it: Can I see you?

Yes, I said, and it was arranged swiftly and businesslike, so I was meeting you the next day at 6.30 in the bookshop by the station near my work.

And the rest of the day and that tomorrow were consumed. Consumed with the secret thought of you, that was venom and cure at once.

At 6.15 in the bookshop, I saw the side of you and felt the fierce thrill of ice down my back. You were reading a reference book and I decided this told me something about you. But as I got closer I saw glazed eyes staring at the stacks and realised it could have been any book at all. You were as isolated by this as I.

You turned around and caught my stare and your face was excitement, sadness and fear. As you walked towards me I watched your whole body exhale and felt my lids fall closed. Then there were arms around me, hips against mine, and your breath, warm, on my neck. I touched the lines of your body through the thinness of your shirt and I wanted to tear it off and scour you with my tongue. Then suddenly your hand was up the underneath of my ponytail, there was a shortness of breath and I was gone; tossed by some indifferent fate into a black, inextricable maze.

But then I opened my eyes and you were there too. There was a kiss on my neck and that hand, again, on the small of my back. We'll find our way out of this, together, you said. And with that we were running, you were holding my hand, and it wasn't so dark anymore. And for a moment, at least, we knew where we were going.

There was a house where we were heading, with lots of windows, a sea view, a big deck and a dog. We built it in our minds and filled it like a dolls' house with the life we'd lead inside.

We craved the ordinary things we thought we were owed. Marmalade with bits in it, peanut butter: crunchy. Good wine, voluptuous couches, a shower set at thirty-eight degrees. Coffee for me, tea for you, roast lamb on Sundays for both of us. A hard bed, soft pillows, crisp sheets and an ocean breeze. And we watched ourselves sleeping, draped with each other, soaked in the peace we gave our fictional selves.

Back on the surface, we'd found hours in the day I didn't know existed and carefully slotted each other in. Privacy was hard though, and people in the obscure meeting places yelled: Puppy love! and: Aren't you finished? and the odd person referred to me as your wife. But we laughed and promised each other this was just a taste of what would come.

A stolen afternoon, a cold, plastic café, far enough removed from our real lives to be safe. I was warming my hands on coffee, you were warming yours on tea. The moments were ticking until we had to say goodbye, and we were cramming in details, learning histories. Learning things with no consequence at all, anything we could grasp to make the other more real.

Quick, quick, favourite soup? I asked

Pea and ham. You?

Minestrone. Favourite ride?

Roller-coaster, you said.

Me too. And the dodgems.

Biggest fear? you asked.

Tunnels.

Me, you said, mediocrity.

Favourite all time moment?

Now.

Reality had escaped us and we dreamt alive the possibility of a reset button, but the best thing, we decided, would be the 'Pause' on a life remote control. All we'd need would be transport and food, and we laughed as we imagined ourselves running through this time-frozen planet: it was you and me, a pilot, a chef and the world.

A lunch hour, sitting in a doorway, cradling my phone. I told you about the lobster sellers on a Cambodian beach. You told me about the time, a year ago, you'd spent two nights in a hotel, convincing yourself to be brave. But your wife was away at her sister's at the time, and by the time she'd got home you'd chickened out, returned home, unpacked your bags, and she still didn't know you'd ever been gone.

In my alone life I was detached and wishing the days away. I couldn't tell a soul but it was too much to contain so I let it grow steadily over the rest of my life. I hadn't spoken to my family for weeks and my studio flat was a mess. I lied to my friends that I couldn't see them because I had too much work, then I'd spend hours staring blankly at my computer screen. And I was hungry, so hungry, for as hard as I tried I couldn't find the room inside for the enormity of us and food as well. My workmates were watching me, curious, but they didn't know me well enough to make me transparent. I was changed. For you'd mined the stale ground of all I knew and exposed the possibility of a thousand first times.

A damp Sunday, I was spending it on the couch, screening my calls, thinking about you; yearning for the Sundays we would spend together. Weekends were long without you, and hard work battling the thoughts of what you were doing, at that moment, with her. I dozed. I dreamt. It would be fixed soon, you promised.

Monday rolled around with its golden glow and I waited for your call.

Hello! I said.

It's a girl.

You told me you'd spent yesterday afternoon with her sleeping on your chest, that she looked just like you, that she was incredible. That you couldn't believe half of her was you.

The violence of our intentions overwhelmed me. Something had to be done. We did it, together, immediately. And with hollow voices, hollow voices, agreed that it was best.

**

Sometimes, now, I stumble across you, both wandering the lost city of our imagined life. You put your hand on the small of my back and lead me home. And there's our house, still standing, built out of nothing but imaginings just to keep each other near.

We sit on the balcony, look out to sea. I drink coffee, you drink tea.

I DREAM OF GAZA

Sarah K Balstrup

Simon was still dressed as an Orthodox Jew and I could see the narrow pass from the shadows where we crouched. They had a temporary ceasefire once every couple of hours, and we had to make it across the border within the specified ten-minute gap. I checked my watch for the hundredth time, and nudged Simon to duck and run, because otherwise we'd never make it home. I covered my shoulders with a thin black veil and we ran with Simon's white chequered scarf flying in our wake.

Palestine was a mess. Hard, flat, desert sand stretched in all directions, cobbled with cement blocks, which must have been the remains of a city. Sand hissed and swirled through the blinding heat, while weary, dust covered figures milled around. The whole place had the air of a refugee camp, but there were no tents, and no aid workers anywhere. Simon and I walked cautiously, not knowing who to speak to, until a young mother found us and took us to her home.

I was surprised when we reached it by merely turning around and walking two metres from where we had been standing. Cramped into a tiny cement bunker, about one metre squared, she proceeded to make us coffee. Pushing back her scarves, the soft luminosity of her skin seemed to highlight the harshness of everything outside. Her warmth and youth would lay exposed to the corrosive winds of war, ceaseless and gritty with sand, while my escape lay imminent. Homes, she explained, had been reduced to their essential element — the kitchen. Without food, they would expire quicker than struck matches. As long as their kitchens stood, families could huddle around them; even if it meant they had to sleep outside like dogs.

Stirring a teaspoon of coffee into the cup of boiling water, she apologised, 'I hope this is okay, you see we cannot get real coffee at the moment, you understand, so we must make do with battle ash.' She paused to see if I would be offended, but I was grateful for her hospitality, and continued to sip from the steaming cup with reverence and sincere appreciation.

I gave her a reassuring smile, and said, 'As long as it's hot enough, anything tastes good. You really can't tell.'

Just then, the boys came home, hot-faced and grimy from the battlefield. The father acknowledged me with a nod while the brothers scrambled past to divulge the latest atrocities.

'They blew him to pieces! Tomorrow, they will see how many of them are splattered on the walls!' Hysteria and testosterone wafted over me in a gust of warm sweat, tinged with the tang of blood and the salt of muddied tears. It lurched over me in a blur, like a heatwave, and I grasped the first brother's arms, partly to steady myself.

I sought him with a look so earnest it gave him a start. 'Violence doesn't solve anything!' I proclaimed. I loaded each word with such weight that the letters bowed like tent beams under wet woollen blankets. It was like screaming from a bridge with fierce winds washing words from your mouth as they formed. He looked at me, pityingly, opening his mouth wordlessly, knowing that I couldn't possibly understand what it was like.

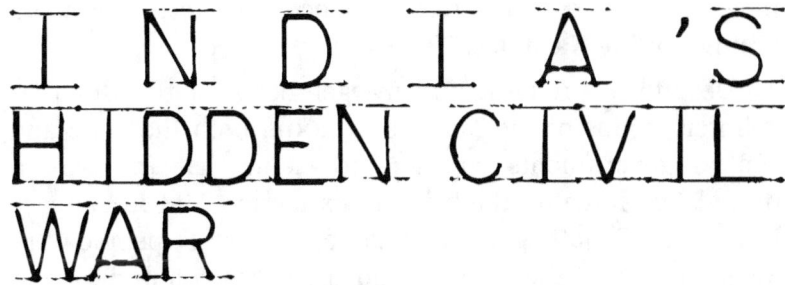

INDIA'S HIDDEN CIVIL WAR

Chris Brown

Travel through the central Indian state of Chhattisgarh, the so-called 'ground zero' of the continuing battle between government forces and Maoist insurgents, and you quickly learn that the little red book of China's Chairman is a long way from the junkyard of political history. This conflict might not attract the headlines of Kashmir, but it is threatening the delicate fabric of contemporary Indian society — a fabric woven from large-scale economic reforms that have delivered unbelievable financial growth to some and complete destruction to others.

Although the Naxalite movement began in 1967 in the small West Bengal town called Naxalbari, it has since shifted its power base to the forested districts of Jharkand, Orissa, Andhra Pradesh and Chhattisgarh and operated largely on a platform of tribal empowerment. It may come as no surprise that these areas are classed as India's most 'backward' and the Indigenous populations that live here are the country's most impoverished. Low employment, destruction of traditional ways of life and an inability to access methods for change has meant that these 'tribal areas' have become a fertile breeding ground for the Naxalites.

Despite a strengthening merger between the different splinter groups of the Maoists in 2004, both the state and central governments continue to claim that they are a diminished force on the brink of extinction. But in January of 2009 in Chhattisgarh state alone, at least 29 people were killed as part of the conflict, and the death count shows no sign of slowing.

Amidst this violence there is one very important question that is begging to be asked: why? Why has the rejected ideology of a dead Chinese man gained such traction in India's hinterlands that it is challenging the strength of an elected government? I wonder if the well-to-do government officials seriously asked themselves this question, what an honest set of answers would be.

A study carried out by the Indian Centre for Science and Development has highlighted an amazing similarity between the booming industrial regions of India and the areas with a strong Naxalite presence. The deregulation of India's economy has led to an influx of multinational mining giants who have all arrived with 'guarantees' of employment and growth, impressive manifestos of corporate social responsibility, and the vocal support of the state governments who promise compensation and resettlement packages for those unwillingly displaced from their land. These developments, they say, will enhance livelihoods and economies through the much touted 'trickle-down' effect to the poor. But increasing discontent within these communities and the continual degradation of traditional environments has led some to argue that the only thing 'trickling down' from the mining industries is a dwindling and polluted water supply.

Displacement figures from 1951–1990 suggest that over 2.5 million people have been displaced in India due to mining projects. Of this number, over fifty percent are Adivasi, an alarming figure when you consider that they make up only eight percent of the general population. And what of those alluring promises made by the corporate giants and democratic governments regarding employment and money? Out of the 1.25 million Adivasi displaced by mining activity, less than a quarter have been compensated and resettled. The government's neglect is shown no clearer than in north-western Orissa where people who were displaced fifty-three years ago due to the creation of the Hirakud Dam have still seen no form of compensation. Their continual attempts for economic justice have now been explained by a lack of record keeping, which means their claims can now not be verified. Just a small scratch of the surface and it becomes hard to ignore the Naxalite claims of government negligence as simply empty propaganda and meaningless rhetoric.

In 2009 the nation of India will take to the polls to either retain the Congress's Manmohan Singh as Prime Minister or elect the BJP's LK Advani. But with Singh, a major architect of India's economic boom, and Advani, a hardline Hindu fundamentalist, it looks like nothing much will change for the Adivasi and the policies that are leading to their destruction. A failure and inadequacy of contemporary electoral politics, Arundhati Roy described thus: 'It's not a real choice. It's an apparent choice. Like choosing a brand of detergent. Whether you buy *Ivory Snow* or *Tide*, they're both owned by Proctor & Gamble'. Consistently denied any participation in decision-making processes, the Naxalites have easily stepped in to fill this major governance gap.

So are the Naxalites our righteous and heroic defenders of social justice and equality? There is of course the typical Communist manifestos that draw a response of 'it's a good idea in theory' from middle-class parents in the 'burbs', but what are their actions? Early in their activities the Naxals gained support and popularity by helping landless peasants reclaim land rights from the exploitative land-owning and money lending classes. They continue to this day to provide an alternative administrative and community structure that includes children's groups and even educational dance performances. And in February of this year they burnt the cement mixer of a private contractor who had failed to pay wages to his labourers. If one stopped here in the Naxalite analysis, we might almost believe that India has its very own Robin Hood prancing around in tights amidst all those colourful saris.

The Naxalites also claim a lack of justice and point to the corruption of police officials who refuse to receive a complaint without a bribe, something that poor farmers simply cannot afford. In response, the Naxals have developed the *Jan Adalat*, a kangaroo court, which supposedly delivers impartial findings, but seems to execute many more than it acquits. On top of this they target public infrastructure for bomb blasts, loot and burn buses plying the night-time routes of rural India and in 2009, in Chhattisgarh alone, have allegedly slit the throats of over ten suspected informers and left their dead bodies as a warning outside each of the family homes.

The relevant governments have responded with force and implied that the Naxalite rebellion is a law and order issue that can be beaten into submission. Sure, they might mention the need for socio-economic development and throw a few million rupees for an electricity project into the hands of corrupt local officials, but these developments are so shortsighted, so misguided and so poorly implemented that their effect is non-existent. In the town of Kashipur in Orissa, the developments from mining activity have not been wealth and employment, but rather it has brought plans for a new gaol to be built to house the many Adivasi who continually protested against the degradation of their traditional land.

The Chhattisgarh government's response has been so heavy-handed that it's been universally condemned by human rights groups as well as the Indian Supreme Court. This approach has seen the active recruitment of child soldiers into front line ranks and the creation of a state sponsored vigilante group known as the Salwa Judum, which, ironically, translates to 'peace mission'. To date, the major contribution of the Salwa Judum to 'peace' has been the forced removal of 100,000 villagers from their traditional farming lands and into camps under their control. Interestingly, there are reports that the Salwa Judum movement was officially launched within twenty-four hours of the Chhattisgarh government signing a memorandum of understanding with Tata steel for an expansion of their operations into the areas from which the villagers were being moved.

Other contributions from the government-employed security forces have been the brutal torture and murder of those suspected to have Naxalite sympathies. This approach of 'erring on the side of violence' was highlighted on 8 January 2009 when nineteen innocent villagers were shot dead in the small village of Singawaram by drunken security forces. Before these farmers were lined up and killed, the women were raped and then made to dress in Naxalite uniforms at gunpoint. An action explained by the Super Intendant of Police, who has admitted that officers are promoted depending on how many Naxalites they have killed. Miraculously, five people escaped and conveyed this information to a local non-government organisation who helped the victims' families file a case which is now before the high court of Chhattisgarh. But with those same police forces lingering in Singawaram Village and continually intimidating the victims, it seems unlikely that the justice system will serve those it was designed to protect.

But it's not all bad news; the possibility for peace did sneak its diminutive frame into the violence-ridden proceedings. Early in February the Chief Minister of Chhattisgarh made the rather encouraging comment that 'the bullet has never produced a solution to any problem in the world'. Not to be outdone, the Naxalites responded days later with an offer of peace talks on the proviso that the government created a 'conducive atmosphere and stopped suppressing the tribals' — a clear enough demand, I guess, but a little scant on the exact details. So where did all this talk of peace, love and mungbeans take us?

Well, outspoken members of the government suggested that the Naxal offer was not to be trusted and was merely a ploy to gather time for a resurgence of their efforts. And within a week the same Chief Minister who seemed so against 'the bullet' announced a monumental increase in the budget for security forces and an agreement to the deployment of larger numbers of central security forces.

These approaches they justify by saying that the Naxals are ruthless terrorists who know no other way than violence, an all too familiar argument promoted by Bush and his neo-conservative cronies. But with that sad era thankfully passed, it remains to be seen if our elected leaders have the capacity for a more nuanced approach. Surely we no longer have to stick to that simplistic Bush statement designed to draw a thick line between good and bad: 'either you are with us, or you are with the terrorists'. This statement was designed to deny anyone the chance to question the ethics and efficacy of the government's response to terrorism, and seeks to label anyone who explains and analyses terrorism as someone who condones it. But as the violence continues and resolution seems increasingly elusive, governments must learn that analysis and explanation are necessary if appropriate remedies are to be found.

Despite their constant talk of peace, the government's actions so far have shown a much greater preference for an ideological and military victory, regardless of the death toll. The Chhattisgarh government, in their attempt to counter Naxalism, have succeeded only in escalating the scale of hostilities, introducing more people to the conflict and splitting traditional communities as villagers are forced to align themselves with one side in the hope of safety and security. Whilst calling for the Naxalites to down their weapons and join the political mainstream, they have at the same time ridiculed the Naxalite offer of peace talks. Though not the only required ingredient for peace, dialogue is surely the starting point from which other things may have grown.

Military might is not going to deliver a victory to the government because the Naxalites are not simply a law and order issue. Security forces can shoot a hundred Naxals or even a thousand, but there will always be a thousand more ready to take their place if there are no solutions to the issues that caused them to take up arms in the first place.

JOURNEY OF THE MAGI

Jarrah Sastrawan

Now that you're here, you can stay as long as you like. Our port is friendly and safer than most, and you will be welcomed with untreacherous smiles, because you've earned them, long-suffering voyagers. You say your travels are forced upon you by destiny? Well, that's neither here nor there; at the very least you must join our feast tonight. There will be wine from our finest vineyards, which are world-renowned, you know, and you will not be disappointed by our suckling pig.

Of course, we'll show your men around. You can't be allowed to pass through this country without beholding our green plains, bristling with every crop, our majestic mountains in the north, or the temperate foothills that cascade down from them to the coast. We're proudest of our weather: light springtime showers, and only the sweetest cool winds blow in from the mountains, mingling with the hot salty air from the sea. There are no damp gusts or little whirlwinds here, ever.

Yes, our sky is very blue; that's something we often hear from foreigners. And now that you've noticed, I know exactly what you will say next. You will ask how it can be such a bright, warm day when, as far as you can see, there is no sun in the sky. There are clouds, and blue sky, and sometimes the soft outline of the moon, but that one object is simply absent. You're right, for our land has never had a sun, not in the furthest reaches of our memory. But we're blessed enough without it; ours is among the richest of nations, yet is also at peace most of the time. There's enough light in our kingdom to go around for everyone, and as you can see, the climate does just fine.

No, it is not impossible. Scientists say that light is refracted by the atmosphere from distant lands, so our plants can grow, and that likewise, worldwide convection currents keep our air at this beautiful temperature. Night is not a problem; it goes dark for twelve hours, and then becomes light for another twelve, just like it does in your country. I don't understand the exact details, but all that information is available at the Academy if you want it. Our situation is perfectly consistent with modern scientific thought. No one doubts that we live, and live well, without actually having this ludicrous shining thing hanging above our heads.

I'm sorry, I don't mean to offend. Appreciate, though, how hard it is for my people to understand your attachment to the sun, something we have never seen or experienced. Other strangers have tried to describe it as a great yellow ball, or a circle of fire, but can't you see how silly that seems to us? Like a child's ball up in the air, or some burning sphere of coal; and that is what your lives depend upon, what controls the rain and snow and drought, what swings our entire planet around with its massive gravitational pull? When we hear these stories, coming out of another world, know that only our respect for guests stops us bursting into laughter.

What, you think I'm lying? You say you can prove me wrong ... please, go ahead, no one has tried that before. You say our scientists base their theories on the assumption that the sun does actually exist. That's not quite right. For them, the sun is a construct, a model that makes the calculations easier to visualise, a bit like how we objectify the experience of cold. Cold, after all, is nothing but the lack of movement of atoms; but we talk of it as if it were a thing that is passed on by touch or by the wind. It's simpler for our schoolchildren to imagine a concrete object called The Sun, hidden underneath the horizon, as the ultimate source of the day's light, even if there is no proof for its existence. They take quite a while to accept the fact that the light might have no preceding cause, and that the answers to some of their questions are beyond the realm of science. A few of our explorers have ventured out to the deserts of the east to try and find the sun, but either they disappear out there, or they return with nothing but grandiose descriptions of white heat and gigantic rays and an ineffable, impenetrable, indescribable power that prevented them from reaching their goal. Personally, I'm not convinced.

We should keep going, friends. There are only a few hours of light left, and we have a fair way to go. I guarantee you'll be impressed by our celebrations, our hearty men and silken young women. Don't hesitate to eat and drink as much as you want, for I'm sure that you and your men haven't had a proper meal for months. There's plenty to go around. Lose yourself in the conversation, tell us stories of where you come from, sing for us if you want. And please stop worrying about your sun; it will be waiting for you when you set sail for home again. But whether it will feel the same, to look up at its blindness, to tell the time by the angle it makes with the horizon, knowing that you could live perfectly without it? Well, I don't know at all.

MY LEGATO HEART

Julie Thorndyke

the cello soars
as we glide upwards
along the road
cut deep into
sandstone cliffs

afternoon sun
warms my hand
resting
on your knee —
the rubato section

violins
float in —
we descend
the curving ridge
of Mt White

the cadenza —
vibrating strings surge
we turn the last bend
your smile caresses
my legato heart

NAPALM

Sophie Trevitt

She bruised gum leaves between two fingers absent-mindedly as she walked home — staring at the cracks in the pavement and at the choking weeds. Tiny green warriors surviving the constant pounding of hard heeled boots. Pockets of life in craterous, war torn no-man's-land. She hoped for that resilience.

Sally slid the key into the lock as gently as possible. Pressing her ear against the door as she slowly turned the handle, she strained to hear any stirrings within. Even if they were home, if she could just steal in quietly, pad down the hallway unnoticed, then she would be able to slide her schoolbag off her shoulders and lie on her bed for a few blissful minutes of complete and utter solitude.

Not today.

'Sally!' came echoing down the hallway. The long white corridor was dotted with tasteful paintings of the seaside and gumtrees. Rather than oozing the minimalist sophistication her mother thought a solitary vase or single candlestick displayed, Sally thought they served as an expensive sort of wallpaper — bland but not unappealing to the eye.

'Sally! Are you home?'

Sally shook her head, what a silly question. Of course she was home and, like always, her mother knew exactly where she was. Sally dropped her bag with a satisfying thud and kicked off her shoes before heading down the Persian runway. She could repeat the same sequence blindfolded everyday and still end up in the same spot — next to her mother's white, spotless apron offering her botoxed cheek for Sally to kiss. Like the Pope almost, Sally realised with a quickly swallowed grin.

'What did you do at school today?' her mother asked as she leant back on the granite bench — the muscles in her neck still strung taught. Sally watched in fascination as her mother smiled calmly whilst her fingers strangled the baby carrot dangling over the colander.

'Nothing,' she eventually mumbled, as usual.

'You can't have spent a day doing *nothing!*' Sally's mother's smile became ever so slightly tighter and her face flushed gently from the collarbone up.

Sally sighed. She didn't understand the point of this charade, in fact she didn't understand the point of a lot of things. Why did she have to kiss her mother's porcelain cheek every morning and night, when it was only to be absent-mindedly rubbed clean by her mother's manicured fingers a minute later? Why did her mother wear matching pants-suits with double-breasted jackets when she spent all day behind a desk answering the phone? Who was she dressing for? And why did she have to recount the same monologue to her mother every day when she returned from school?

As Sally pondered, her mother lost interest in her wayward daughter and flicked open her phone. Sally walked to her room and gently shut the door with a small sigh of relief. The game was over.

Sally lay on her bed motionless for some time. She liked the solid stillness of air trapped in a soundproof room. She liked the regular rise and fall of her hands resting on her stomach as she breathed in and out. She liked the way her limbs felt heavy as they sank into the supportive folds of her doona. But she hated the way her mind saw through doors of wood and concrete walls and how, if her eyelids dropped, she would see her mother dancing before her eyes, wielding a knife and laughing in derision as she stabbed, stabbed, stabbed.

Sally opened her eyes. Quickly. She inched her hand up towards her chest and felt her heart beat in her fingers and pound within her head. Sometimes it wasn't the images themselves that scared her, so much as their vitality. Implausible as the snapshots were, they played on the skirting board of possibility and fiction. How would you sponge blood out of a linen suit, Sally wondered ... she could hardly get it dry-cleaned.

Sally savoured solitude. She let it envelope her like others bathed in the laughter and affection of friends. She found comfort in the soft recesses of stillness and silence. Sally knew that most people were scared to be alone but even the inky blackness under her doona was a welcome respite from the thick, suffocating air that permeated the rest of her house. You could almost slice it, like you would thick wedges of cheese.

The dinner bell rang and Sally abruptly opened her eyes. She slapped her cheeks to ensure that she was, in fact, awake before assuming her place at the table. Sometimes she confused her nightmares with reality.

Her life was a ritual. She took her place at the table, between her parents at either end. Her mother, with her amber teardrops and frosted hands, could easily be regal and her father, in his black and white suit and austere expression, heralded a religious air. Sally felt dwarfed by their presences, as though they were sucking the air out of the room and dragging the dregs from her lungs so she slowly deflated until she would be just a pile of clothes.

Sally's mother nodded across the table and the pair clenched their forks simultaneously — the ceremony had begun. Sally leant back in her chair as she watched the metamorphosis — her mother's rings became crusted additions to her gnarled fingers as she clawed at the cutlery. Her head sprouted feathers as she pecked at corn with a sharp, curved beak and squawked occasionally with either frustration or pleasure, it was hard to tell. The only thing that didn't change were her hard black eyes that seared the steak if she eyed it too long — and filled the kitchen with that only too familiar acrid smell of burning.

Sally turned to see her father crouching on the table. Holding the corn cob with two paws he gnawed it determinedly. All the while his eyes darted left and right as if wary of predators or perhaps scanning for prey.

A loud crunching prompted Sally to divert her attention back to her mother who was grinding the T-bone with the corner of her beak, having wiped the rest of her plate clean. All of a sudden a gleam flicked across those hard black ember eyes and she flew at Sally in a flurry of feathers and colour and sunk her talons into Sally's arm.

Sally had no time to react. She watched in horror as her mother proceeded to tear at her flesh. Sally flashed a desperate glance across to her father, whose weasel eyes flicked back and forth before he resumed his devouring of the cob.

Spying the fleshy red protrusions from Sally's face, her mother pieced Sally's lower lip with a satisfied squawk. Tasting the rush of blood and the hot flood of pain Sally blindly thrashed and kicked until she threw off her attacker in a cloud of feathers and ran into her room.

She pressed her back against the door and felt it creak and curve to hold her upright in a show of sympathy. Her bed inched closer, the doona peeled back and her lamp dimmed softly. If wood could cry, Sally had no doubt the whorls in the grain would be leaking tears.

She sat on the edge of her bed in front of her mirror. Her lip was pierced right through and stained purple, as if she had been sucking bloody mulberries. Her arms were torn and fingers shredded from where she tried to shield her face. The mirror bent and curved away, as if shielding her from herself. Sally gave up and sunk into the warm recesses of her bed.

Sometimes she thought she could hear it crackling, or see tiny wisps of curling smoke. The caustic stench of burnt toast seemed to linger in the fabric of the couch and the curtains' heavy folds. It was most pungent, though, at the door to her parents' room. Sally wondered how her mother could sleep in a burning bed, maybe that's why her eyes were so frequently red and watery when she said goodbye to Sally on her way to school.

This morning, like any other, Sally was preparing lunch for school. Sally took great pains to pack her lunch — she liked the idea of packaging and controlling every portion. She evenly spread a thin layer of butter on a Vita-Weat then a thinner still coat of vegemite. Continuing until she had a neat stack of five Vita-Weat sandwiches, Sally wrapped them in gladwrap and placed them snugly between her carrot sticks and cold, hardboiled egg — prepared the night before.

As Sally arranged her books in accordance with her timetable (English went in last because it was first period, then French, Maths and double Latin) her mother strode into the bathroom. Sally was slightly disturbed by her mother's daily ritual of transformation. Make-up was not a tool to enhance her facial features, rather it was a thick coat of paint intended to disguise, even create an entirely different face. Bleary, red eyes were rimmed in thick black and eyelashes were painstakingly stuck on; the face was doused in dark foundation that covered blemishes but also filled every line and crevice with a thick layer of plaster; her earlobes were tugged and stretched by chandeliers and her mouth smeared red. That was what Sally hated most — that angry, red hole that opened and closed to spit out violence and pain and distorted truth.

'Bye, mum,' Sally muttered through a mouthful of peanut butter and a quick gulp of tea. The red slashed mouth opened and closed in response but Sally already had her headphones in, blocking out the world.

Sometimes Sally felt powerful striding along with her headphones in her ears and a fag in her mouth. Sometimes, she felt like she was encased in an invisible, bulletproof bubble. People would charge at her, hit the invisible barrier and be thrown back onto the dust. In the safety of her bubble she was almost brave enough to laugh. She didn't though, she knew that if someone struck at just the right angle her bubble would burst — if they charged with just the right amount of malice and venom then her wall would simply dissolve away and she would be left to fend for herself against the elements.

Sally pulled out a cigarette as she slammed the gate shut behind her, wrinkling her nose at the unpleasant smell. She stopped behind the station to light up, flicking and flicking and flicking until a tiny flame caught flight and she breathed in deeply. The smoke coursed through her windpipe and into her lungs. She closed her eyes and watched the embers glow on the fringes of her alveoli: tiny fronds of flame spreading, like miniature bush fires in her lungs, eating away the flesh and leaving charred remnants. Sally put out the cigarette on her arm, burning away the peck marks and leaving tiny, perfect black circles in their place.

Sally rolled in her invisible sphere into school. She skirted on the edges of crowds, rolled into class just seconds late so she could lurk in the background invisible and impenetrable. Then softly, in the sanctity of the classroom, she unzipped her bubble and folded it into her bag. She was safe. School was her refuge. Her classmates, her teachers were like beacons of light. She loved the idea of school, of people gathering to learn — like cavemen sitting around a fire warming their hands and listening to ancient stories of hidden dangers and of truth. She loved to rule up red margins and write in black ink on white — deciphering texts and decoding maths problems.

She loved the safety of school routine. The teacher walked in and chairs scraped back as the students stood to attention and Sally silently rejoiced in the knowledge that no metamorphosis would take place — that her teacher would remain in his jeans and white shirt and her peers would stay in their pressed uniforms and ribbons all day. She was not invisible at school but it was the one place that she did not mind being seen, she knew she would not be seared by her teacher's concerned gaze and she knew that a flicked note would contain no more than the weekend's news or a piece of delightful gossip. There was enough air for everyone to breathe easily and to laugh and talk. Sally wasn't scared here.

Mr Brunsten sat down and, on cue, soft banter erupted as the class sat and settled into the day. They were studying *King Lear* in English. Sally placed her play on her desk with almost reverential care as she smoothed the cover and opened it to page twenty-seven, where they had left off. Another world was trapped in the pages and Mr Brunsten was the key to releasing the voices in the ink; Sally worshipped him for that.

'Sally, would you like to start?'

Sally smiled with quiet exaltation as she began to read the words of the broken hero. She felt herself transcend her schoolyard existence as she spoke the words of a man torn apart with insecurity and desperation for love. She felt her heart ache in unison with his as she begged her daughters to spare her dignity and her power; she felt her eyes well with tears as she watched Lear fall to his knees in a last, anguished gesture of desperation. Sally choked as her eyes were seared with the same bitter hurt as Lear's and her pain translated into rage. She unknowingly rose as she cursed Goneril, her daughter, and called on Nature to condemn her to a life of barren solitude. Sally felt the power of his words, his wrath, tear at her soul as she rejected her own flesh and blood that had so painfully wronged her.

'Very good, Sally,' Mr Brunsten's voice gently penetrated Sally's consciousness and she allowed herself to sink back to reality and blush with schoolgirl satisfaction.

Elise squeezed her still trembling arm, 'You're so good at this!' Sally smiled back, and felt the bruises on her arm begin to heal under the friendly hand.

Sally looked up at Mr Brunsten with frank adoration and he looked down at her with such warm respect that she thought she would melt. It was not so much a crush as gratitude that dissolved her. He so quietly and simply validated her very being and she knew she could never thank him for it.

For his part, Mr Brunsten was taken aback by the strength of Sally's passion. He had never seen Shakespeare resonate so profoundly with someone of her age. Most fourteen-year-olds were hindered by the convoluted language and struggled with the abstract themes of love and betrayal, but Sally seemed to dredge emotion from somewhere deep within her and pour it out in his classes. He was sometimes almost embarrassed watching her speak. It was like she was bleeding on the desk in front of him and he could only observe. He felt that she was sharing something deeply personal, even though she never moved past the four-hundred-year-old script.

Mr Brunsten cleared his throat and reshuffled his notes. English always caught him slightly off guard; he was never prepared for its intensity. 'Okay, girls, settle down. If you turn to Act III Scene IV we are going to deconstruct Lear's monologue.'

Sally allowed herself to relax into a quiet state of ecstasy. Language was the most incredible, beautiful thing. As she circled similes and highlighted metaphors she felt as though she was running her fingers over the intricacies of a finely woven tapestry — admiring each perfect stitch before stepping back in awe and gazing at the mirage in front of her.

Language, Sally marvelled, was timeless. We write books and poetry not to be read just by our contemporaries but, so that in years to come, someone can blow the dust from its thumbed cover and rediscover the power of the thoughts and feelings trapped in the yellowing pages. Language allows us to reach out to those around us, and speak of the invisible forces that unleash havoc in our innards; but it also allows us to seek solace in the understanding that someone has felt what we feel before, that no emotion is new and no challenge unconquered. In language, Sally found hope. Hope that she too could survive and achieve greatness like the heroines on paper did time and time again. That's why words were so precious to her, they were her lifeline.

'Excellent work, Sally.'

Sally blinked and brought her eyes back into focus. She realised, as a flush of red hit her neck, that her eyes were swimming. She quickly wiped her face on her jumper sleave as discretely as she could.

'Come and see me after class, Sally.'

Mr Brunsten had leant down so he could speak softly and not add to her ill ease, but she could feel his breath stir every hair on her neck and she shuddered involuntarily. He looked at her swiftly and added, 'You're not in trouble.'

Sally spent the rest of the lesson trying to breathe. She wanted to talk to him desperately. She wanted to cut out her heart and give it to him for safekeeping. Some of the kids gave him their medicine at the beginning of term, and each day he'd give them the tablets for that morning and then put the jar of pills away. She wished he could keep her heart in his cabinet and give it to her each day so she could feel her pulse alongside Lear's; and then take it back before she left so only her thick, outer shell would bear the signs of wear and tear from life in a war zone.

But she was too scared. What if she cut open her chest and there was nothing there? What if her mother was right and, instead of a child with a beating heart of youth and compassion, she had a greying cavity, a burnt-out canyon where maggots nested. No wonder her mother couldn't love her. No, she couldn't risk Mr Brunsten seeing that.

Sally spent Maths with her left hand resting on her chest. She pressed her fingers into her flesh through the coarse material of her checked uniform and she prayed for shoots of life to sprout where her fingers touched. As she wrote down rows of perfectly formed numbers and indented rows of working, she hoped that, somehow, the beauty of their symmetry and their logic would jolt some of her dead cells into life.

Sally's desperation was interrupted by the chiming of the recess bell. Usually, Sally loved this moment. She loved watching the room of quiet order and concentration disintegrate momentarily into one alive with squeals and writhing young bodies before, in seconds, it was completely vacated. Today, the bell rang and Sally was washed with a cold fear. What did Mr Brunsten want? Would he see right through her? Did he know she was a fraud?

'Sally,' his voice was warm and kind. Sally unclenched her eyes and realised that everyone had left and it was only her in the second row and her teacher. Mr Brunsten nodded for her to come up to his desk, so Sally slid down off the chair and waded through the wood and steel.

'Sally,' he smiled down at her. Sally always marvelled at how teachers managed to smile down at you in that warm safe way, even when they were sitting and you were standing. Sally looked at him carefully; you didn't often get to really look at a teacher. He was wearing blue jeans and, because he was crossing his legs, she could see a tiny strip of yellow where his pants had pulled up to reveal his socks. The jeans, combined with his crisp white shirt (top buttons undone), were what gave him his reputation amongst the older girls for being a bit of a hunk.

'Are you listening to me, Sally?'

Sally pulled her eyes up to his and instantly regretted having done so. His eyes were still kind, still warm, but she hadn't missed the flash of irritation that crossed over them.

'Sorry, sorry,' she stammered. That hunger came back into her eyes and Mr Brunsten coughed awkwardly. His eyes flicked above her head and when their eyes reconnected he was once again composed.

'That's quite alright, Sally, I imagine you want to be at recess with your friends.' Sally did quite like recess — she liked pulling out her Vita-Weat soldiers and eating them one by one in quick succession (or slowly if it was a rainy day — because things are to be savoured when the world is damp and heavy).

'I am a bit worried about you, to be honest.'

Worried. Sally's brain processed this quickly. Worried was not the same as concerned. 'I'm concerned about your work,' 'I'm concerned about your daughter's attitude.' No, concerned was not the same as worried. Sally felt a tiny burst of life where she thought her heart should go — worried meant he cared.

'Your work is excellent, *too* excellent almost. You pay attention and don't talk in class. Your love for English, Sally, is ... unusual for someone of your age.'

Sally waited. She knew something was coming. She stood with her hands folded on the corner of his desk and bit the inside of her mouth. He couldn't have talked to her mother; he most certainly would not be sitting so comfortably near her if he knew who she really was. Maybe he'd found out himself. Teachers can see things that other people can't. Mr Brunsten saw when Sandra sticky taped a tampon to Freya's back and he didn't even turn around. Maybe he just looked at her and saw right through her, like an X-ray. Next to all these girls with pink fleshy lungs and rosy hearts, she'd stood out as a black hollow shell.

'Is something happening at home, Sally? Something that's upsetting you?'

Sally looked up in surprise. At home? She looked down at her arms but the peck marks had already healed over. They always seemed to do that at school. At home they were red and raw and bloody, but the skin fused every day when she sat down at her desk and immersed herself in different tongues and different worlds.

Mr Brunsten leant forward slightly. He'd been watching the turmoil in her face as she stood their silently — flashes of distress and a grimace of pain. 'Sally,' he said with a new urgency, 'Sally, you can tell me if there's something wrong.'

She stood there staring at the wall. With her backpack on and her slightly too big uniform she looked even younger than she was. Mr Brunsten was taken aback by the surge of emotion that hit him. He stood up and walked around his desk so there was no longer a barrier between them.

'Sally,' he put his hand on her shoulder. Sally almost crumpled under the sheer weight of having someone care about her. Her arms burned where there had once been injuries and her chest ached. She shook her head again and again to try and shake out the images. It felt like his hand was pressing deeper and deeper into her, like he was plunging into the crevices of her soul. She was overcome by a cold, hard fear that he would see all that she had seen. That he would see her mother stab, stab, stabbing and laughing in mad derision; that he would watch her at the table as she was suffocated and fought for air ... Sally turned and fled.

Sally hesitated at the front door that afternoon. She glanced down at her shoulder. She could still feel the imprint of his hand on her skin. She wondered if her mother would know — if her nose would burn with the smell of something different from the usual stench of death and singed flesh.

Sally slid the key into the lock and braced herself. She would have to draw his touch, his warmth deep in her if she was going to protect it from the flames. Subconsciously, Sally hunched her shoulders as if sheltering something fragile, something precious at the centre of her being.

Tiptoeing into the house, Sally felt it in her fingers first. A tingling that heralded danger, like the heat from a fire when you warm your hands too close. Then she felt it on her face. Hot, dry pulses that made her eyes smart and water and seared the insides of her nostrils. Sally dropped to her hands and knees and crawled down the hallway. She couldn't see any smoke but she knew it was there — mixing with oxygen to form a deadly invisible gas.

Face prickling, she crawled into her bedroom and put her shoes and bag on her bed, just in case the flames should snake up the bedposts. She waited for her mother to beckon.

She sat with her knees pulled into her chest and her toes curled under. Time passes so slowly when you're waiting for an explosion. Her ears were straining and eyes stretching to pick up the even tiniest warning of what was to come. The smoke was making her dizzy and she could feel it clogging the whorls of her ears. So she unfolded herself and crept down the hallway.

She hesitated at the kitchen door, half expecting to see her parents passed out on the floor. For a second she imagined that the crime scene was unveiled and two bodies were splayed on the ground, swollen and puffy from all the gas. She was surprised at the bolt of fear that shot through her at the thought. Closing her eyes, she could see her mother's face and dried blood caked around her nose. She watched herself kneeling next to her mother's body, holding the cold white hand that so readily grew talons, and realised she was weeping.

Sally shook her head and stepped around the kitchen door.

Two statues were seated at the table. Smoke licked their feet and curled up the stone bases to swirl around their legs. They had been waiting, Sally realised. Their lives had stopped and turned to stone.

Her mother's marble exterior began to crack as she lifted the teacup to her lips and a trail of marble dissolved where the tea trickled down her throat. As her father turned over a page of the newspaper, hairline fractures appeared up and down his arm and slowly their stone casings began to peel off.

'Sally,' her mother spoke, dangerously calm as she shook plaster fragments from her hair, 'We had a call from school today.'

Sally's father peeled a stray flake of cement from his jaw.

Sally stared at her mother's mouth and imagined her stone jaw grinding her teeth into powder.

'Do you know what we got a call about, Sally?'

Sally was distracted by the smoke. Couldn't her parents see all the smoke? It was burning her throat.

Sally could feel her mother's eyes boring into her and, with horror, she realised her legs were growing heavier and her arms were already fixed to the chair.

'Apparently there is something wrong at home, Sally,' her mother continued quietly, her voice laced with a barely contained venom. As her eyes roamed over Sally's body she felt her arms and legs deaden and turn cold. They had been waiting hours as stone-cold statues and now, Sally realised, it was her turn to be immobilised.

She thrashed momentarily before pressing back in the chair as far from her mother as possible. Her torso was free to flounder helplessly but her limbs were too heavy to lift. She tilted her head back and tried to breathe the clearer air higher up but her lungs were aching and she was scared to leave her neck so exposed.

'Is there something wrong at home? Something wrong with the way we feed you? Clothe you? Provide for you?' The words were coming quick and fast but, as the cold feeling crept up Sally's neck and mouth, she found she could not reply. She could only move her eyes from side to side and watch with terror as her mother's mouth opened again and a red forked tongue rolled out. It flicked in and out.

As her mother's face elongated and flattened, Sally saw a dark shape slide behind her from the corner of her eye. Her mother's nose was compressed into two slits and her yellow eyes narrowed. Green tinged her skin and Sally soundlessly screamed as a twin serpent twined its way around her mother's throat and they coiled and uncoiled in a sadistic dance.

When their eyes fixed on her with such ravenous hatred, Sally had no doubt she was the field mouse frozen rigid with fear. A forked tongue ran down her neck and Sally bucked furiously against the chair but her arms and legs remained motionless. Her torso was pushed forward as a thick, muscular body snaked its way behind her back and around, wrapping her in a grip that she knew would slowly tighten and crush the air from her lungs.

Sally had watched nature documentaries with a sick fascination as field mice were slowly crushed by the lean body of a boa constrictor. She had watched for entertainment as tiny bones broke and warm bodies went cold, and she had watched as fanged monsters devoured corpses whole. Sally imagined her own body as a lump bloating the snake's belly, slowly being dissolved by acid. She froze and her world was doused in napalm.

SAYING

Ian Steep

Saying 'I love you' has always been a problem for me. Not so much the actual saying but *when* I say it. Those three words, that contestants on reality and TV soap shows throw around like pillows decorating a couch, seem to get stuck in my throat when I'm with someone I really like but are blurted out with abandon in the middle of the most casual encounters. The consequences can be painful.

Take Pete. I answered an ad on *Pinkboard*. 'No strings, casual.' Sounded good to me. I was holding together a stagnant relationship that worked well as a domestic economy but not much more. But it worked. Sort of. There was no sex but after fifteen years, who expects it? So the thought of some no strings, casual sex looked like a reasonable option.

We met at the ANA in the Rocks; his hotel. Even better — an out-of-towner. No chance of getting caught up in something I wasn't looking for. We talked for a while in the lobby then went to his room where the sex was unexciting but enough to break the ice that had built up over the last ten years. He was leaving town the next day so we did the right thing: shared a beer from the minibar and said goodbye.

The beer was probably the first mistake. According to the rules, you fuck then leave. But not having dated for longer than most people could imagine, I had no idea. Casual sex outside a relationship was new to me.

A week later Pete was back. We arranged to meet, as before, at his hotel. This time in the Cross. The Kirketon looked like a fetish hotel. Dark walls, low lights. Low-on-the-floor lights that gave the corridor a sense of something nasty. Opening the door, Pete was as I remembered: no chains, no leather, just a guy. But in a bathrobe apparently ready for the old casual, no strings. Yep, suited me.

This time the sex was better and there was an unmistakable sense of intimacy. At least I thought so. That's when I said it.

'I love you.'

A moment passed. Pete withdrew. (Oops.) Not too much but definitely.

'I thought this was about no strings,' he said.

'I don't mean I love you *forever*,' I said, trying to explain to him and myself what I meant, 'I mean, just for now. Just for this moment.'

And it was true. That's what I meant. For that moment or the hour or however long I felt it, I did love him.

And that's where the problem starts. It's not so much the words but what they mean.

Pete and I saw each other on a casual, no strings basis for another six months or so. He always stayed at good hotels and we ate in expensive restaurants. He would go shopping at Prada or Armani and ask what I wanted but I never accepted his offers. When he wasn't in town we kept in touch by email. In one of those emails, written at five in the morning and drunk after a long night of work, he told me he loved me.

Not long after, he dumped me. By phone. He said he had got me too involved in his life and that we should cool it. I was standing in the rooftop car park at the Marrickville Metro when I heard it. That was it: 'Cool it'. I didn't understand he meant 'end it'. I thought I had misunderstood him.

Some time later, after too many tears and well-meant but ultimately useless advice from friends, acquaintances and anyone who would listen, I posted a message on *Pinkboard*. I wanted to know what others understood by those words. What did they mean when they said 'I love you'? What did they understand when someone said it to them?

More than three hundred people opened the message but there were only seven replies. And no two the same. One took the time — the *long* time — to explain the difference between *eros* and *agape*. Another wrote about springtime in Paris. And another wrote about the pain of walking out because it was simply time to leave.

I wasn't much further ahead, but what I did learn was that when it comes to love we're not all talking the same language. What one person says isn't necessarily what another person hears.

So what did I mean when I told Pete I loved him? On reflection, I think I meant he made me feel good. But was that enough reason to use those three words that carry all the commitment and passion that Hallmark cards and countless women's magazines would have us believe?

And for me, that's the scary part. That's why, when I really care, I'm afraid to say it. Because of the expectations it sets up and because I don't want the other person thinking that I'm offering more than I'm prepared to give. I don't want to offer a Tiffany 'I love you' and have the other person think it came from Kmart.

I never found out from Pete what he meant when he wrote his email at five in the morning. After he dumped me his mobile was disconnected and he refused to answer my emails. Or maybe he just didn't get them. And in the end, does it matter? Maybe it was just Kmart in a Tiffany box. But it felt good at the time.

SKIES AND
CLOUDS AND
SUCH

Rowan McKay

In her endless vaulted empire
Lolls the languid sun.
A kookaburra bursts with joy;
The day has just begun.

The dandelions yawn and stretch;
Teasing out the tangled rays
And soaking up their warming glow
To keep for darker days.

As subtle airs of dew and ivy
Laze upon the breeze
That wafts across the old canal
And feathers through the trees

I wander early from my berth
And the many thousand voices worth
Of weary words and pyrrhic mirth.
I head for Epping Station.

My collar catches stiff black whiskers,
Pinching one or two,
And lizards scamper to avoid
The morning's sweeping view.

Slipping through the flotsam
Of that caffeinated stream,
Which leaks out of the Witching Hour's
Syphilitic dream
And trickles down to disappear
Through every crack and seam,

My eye can hardly move before
It's brought once more to rest,
Snared by all the shining threads
Of another sticky nest.

Crisp air pools in the verdant shade
And slithers down my throat
To drip on down, collect and sit
And every drip, it strikes that pit
With an awful jangling note.

I stop to sit and rest my eyes
A while from all the glare
And as they shut I swore a shape
Darkened the upper air.

Ah, shadows dance in open skies
Around a sunny grin
And stir mephitic fumes within
A sheer nocturnal skin

And all the rays pour down on me,
So hot and razor thin,
But on a cloud they might explode;
A mighty pink and orange ode
To joy at ruptured sin.

I scan the heavens for a sign
Of any little cloud
But nothing's there except the sky
All haughty, blue and proud.

STOP

Amanda Taylor

Heartbeat. Stop. Must keep going. No. Where am I? Lost. What's that? Searchlight? No time, have to get away. Where am I going? Don't care, anywhere is better than there.

Was it three years ago, I don't remember? Maybe it was yesterday, how can I be sure? I met him there, I'm sure of that, sure as I am that I live and breathe. Though, I suppose, that too is questionable, now that I know. Sometimes I wish I didn't, it'd be easier not to. I could have been happy there, just like the others. I don't mean to imply that I enjoy pain, or sadness but is life real if you never experience the full spectrum of emotion? I think that's why I'm here now, running from them. I think I need this; I need to find out things for myself, not be told or shown, but feel. In a world of pure happiness is anything ever pure? But what if they are right; I can never go back, not now. Not after what I did. It had to be done really, no two ways about it; it was the only way out. Of course I would have chosen another way if I could, one that didn't cause others to suffer, but it was the first and last pain they would ever have to feel. Their pain lives in me now, in all of us.

It was supposed to be perfection, the height of achievement. The theorists of past times, terrestrial walkers, they had ideals. We made them reality, built the dream, the summit of our species. But in that process we lost so much. Gave it away really; it was never taken, never by force. It was submission, acquiescence that was our downfall. They didn't lie, not once. We knew what we were getting into; we chose it. You would too, if offered the choice. Flawlessness. Isn't that what you want: love, ecstasy, belonging, elation, warmth, an all encompassing embrace? If they offered that to you, to take away all misery, all sadness, all loneliness, would you reject it? Huh, I guess that's what I'm doing now.

I don't even know why I'm telling you this, I know you can't hear me; I may as well be talking to a corpse. You see my words, but hear them in your own voice, in your own head. Like some piece of fiction, a little story to wile away the tedious hours. Stop. This is my life, it's not a fiction, I'm not a fiction, and perhaps it is you who are? This world is real to me, as I'm sure yours is to you. But you have the condescension to consider yourself safe from the horrors of my world. Don't. I sent you this message the only way I could, so they wouldn't see it. I couldn't very well broadcast this to your whole world, they'd stop it, know who it was, never stop hunting me. They probably won't anyway.

But I wanted someone to know, to give us a chance. Maybe it doesn't have to happen, if you stop it. I would tell you more, but there isn't time; it's not safe, for you. When they come, and they will, to your world as they did to mine, stop them. Say no, save yourself, save everyone. I can't tell you how they will come; it's different every time. They came from among us, as if they were always there, as if they were us. And I suppose they were — are — us. I don't know when they came, surely before my inception. I don't remember before. Only after. It was my role to read for us all; we each have functions like that. It was while functioning as reader that I first became aware of it. It was a while before I could control it. Strange really. You see we are all connected through them. We feel together. But to maintain the feelings, functions must be performed. If I was to dysfunction, that is read something and feel bad, I would be disconnected. I knew that, but I didn't know what 'to feel bad' was, until I learned to lie. Lie with feelings. Feel one way, but think another. Then, when I did that, I knew I could try to read forbidden things. I'd known about them, but never dared disobey, the sections of stories blanked out, not removed but hidden. No one had disobeyed before, no one had ever wanted to, I think. They knew that. That's why they never removed the sadness; they knew we didn't want it. But I did. I was just too curious; I think being a reader did that to me. You're a reader too aren't you; I can tell, so you know what I mean, I always wanted to know more.

One day, I did it: felt happy, but thought sad. It was unfulfilling; I wanted more. I wanted to experience the sadness described; most of all I wanted to feel these things called tears. I tried not to want — want intellectually; I knew I could never allow myself to communicate that desire to others. But I kept reading, and the more I read the more I knew I had to get out, get away. I saw my world was wrong. But to disconnect is to die. So we were taught. A one-way process they said. We accepted. But I was not given the choice, though I'm sure I would have gone along anyway. But once I knew, I had to stop, had to be me.

That's when I met him. I knew when I saw him he was like me. In fact I felt it, we all did. Feeling one another's attractions and passions is supposed to make us all less lonely, but secretly, nothing is the same as your own attraction, your own desire being reciprocated by another individual. The emotions of others are nice, but not as nice as your own. You can't share love.

It made it harder to leave; I wanted to stay with him. But to stay was to share, to share him, to share us. In fact that was the problem; too much us, too many of us. I wanted him to come with me. I think he knew that. I hope he did. I couldn't risk it, letting him know. I wasn't sure it wouldn't make him feel something. In the end of course he felt, as they all did.

I only had one shot, one chance to make them all feel as I wanted to. I had to choose a story, just one short story. I choose it for him; if nothing else, I wanted for him to know how it would be for me to leave him. I'm sure they knew immediately. I don't even know how much the other felt, but I know I did. The exquisiteness of the pain, the unbearable agony of the loss, the final heartbreak. I knew it was over when it was all I felt. There was no happiness to mask it, no shared feelings from the others, just my own sorrow. And for the first time, I cried.

Then I ran, I cried and ran. I still feel sad when I think of that. The loneliness, the hurt. But I wanted it, and I wanted you to know. You see, I still have some of what they gave us. Emojection they call it; a way to communicate thoughts and feelings across space and time. For those of us far away. Like you are from me. I don't know why I chose you; only that I felt your mind would understand. You would listen. And you have, all this time. You listened. Know, remember, what I've said, what you've felt. And when they come, make them stop.

THE BALCONY

Vesna Leto

Under the twilight
river strums a song.
The shy moon traces
the ridge
as though it were its lover's backbone.
Moon's breath whispers
over my eyelids
and so I begin to breathe
entering silver shadows, orbiting
above the happiness
of pine and chestnut.

It's how
I've always imagined
the falling
of stars, on a northern summer's night ...

Donkey's slow cobble echoes —
the wolf circles my memories.

THE LADY AND THE BIRD

Mark Yeow

When I was five, my parents bought me a budgerigar to teach me how to be responsible. The first responsible thing to do, of course, was to give the bird a name. So while my parents were in the backyard pouring birdseed into plastic bins I asked him what the other birds knew him as.

'Where I grew up, they called me Jef,' he told me.

When my parents asked me that night what I wanted to name him, I told them his name was Jef. They smiled complacently at how adamant I was that it be spelt with one 'f', not two.

It didn't occur to me until a bit later, when my parents caught me discussing philosophy with my budgie ('Why is the sky blue, Mr Jef?') and started giggling at the cuteness of it all, that not everyone could talk to birds. And birds didn't talk to everyone.

'Why are they laughing, Mr Jef?,' I asked once my parents had sidled away. I was about eight or so; at that age when mother and father's reluctance to take me seriously was beginning to irritate me, like a heavy conker that rolls under your bare feet and jabs at your sole with its dull spikes. Jef never laughed at me; for all his good humour, I don't think I ever heard him laugh at all.

'Not all humans can hear what we birds say,' explained my budgie. 'And out of the few who can, most don't really want to talk to us.'

'Why, Mr Jef?'

'They're too busy? They've forgotten how to dream? I don't know. That's just the way things are.'

'You're funny, Mr Jef,' I told him gravely, and I took him out of his cage and held him in my cupped hands where he gently nibbled at each of my fingers in turn, making sure each one got special attention. It was something he'd done ever since he'd told me his name. But that day I realised it wouldn't be like this forever. When I looked at his feathers I noticed that there brilliant green was just that little bit frayed at the edges. One day Jef and I wouldn't be having these conversations anymore. I squeezed him a little tighter and he turned his bright black eyes to wink at me, like he knew exactly what I was thinking.

'You're funny too, my lady,' he said, and when he whistled his family's anthem, I felt a little better.

He'd told me his life story about six months after I got him. He sat on my shoulder as I lay stomach-down in bed reading about where the wild things used to be.

'I come from an old patrician family of wild budgerigars,' he informed me. 'They reside deep in the outback, where men rarely dare to forage.' He had this special voice he used for telling me stories, where his chest would puff out and he'd use long words which I didn't always know the meaning of but could somehow understand.

'Like the Queen,' I suggested.

'Except more male-dominated, yes. We have a grove of eucalypts, which you might call our palaces, and a hunting-song, which would pass as our regal anthem. I was but a minor prince, though, but all the happier for it, since the burden of leading the flock would never fall to me. I ended up a bit of an adventurer, always swooping amongst our trees, pretending to be a falcon or some other noble bird of prey.

I often went exploring and would pass over many desolate regions where naught but scorpions, black and shiny as pitch, crawled, and just as many oases, where bilbies and skinks and all forms of life struggled to survive and make good for their families. But one day I flew too far and strayed into dangerous skies, where an eagle spotted and tore at me with talons sharp as the desert heat. It would have consumed me had not a snake then menaced its nearby nest. I bear it no grudge, mind you. We must all live in such a fashion, never knowing when a fiercer and more agile creature will snatch life away in its grasp. When I was discarded, I lay by the roadside for many hours until some humans found and tended for me. But they did not let me return to my kin.'

'But you can fly back, Mr Jef,' I said, and I even got up to open my bedroom window. I held him out to the star-drenched sky. 'Can't you?'

'My wings are crook,' he muttered in his ordinary voice, 'and I could never fly that far in any case. Besides,' and he lay his head against my pyjamas, 'it wouldn't be right to run away'.

One night, when all the lights were out and my mother and father could be heard snoring in tandem, he asked me, 'Do you dream much, my lady?' He never called me anything but that. Not Ellie or El, like my friends and not Elsie like my parents. His patrician upbringing, I suppose.

'Sometimes,' I told him, 'but I usually forget.'

'Can you ever remember falling asleep?'

I had to think about this one. I've thought about it many times since then, when lying alone in bed after a tough week's work and when drifting off woozily in the back of cabs in foreign cities. I just don't know anymore.

'You can't,' was what I said to Jef. 'Otherwise you'll never fall asleep. You'll just keep waiting and you'll be up all night.' I thought it was some sort of test, like the ones that we got at school now that my friends and I were in Year 5. I guess it was, in a way.

'There is a myth amongst my kin that if you can pinpoint the exact moment when you go from conscious to unconscious, the moment when time and sleep collide, you can control where your dreams take you. And that those dreams will come true.'

He said this slowly, like he expected me to laugh or refute him and then fell into a deep silence. I did not break it.

'I've been trying for months,' he finally admitted, 'but I can't do it. I just can't.'

And he shook his head from side to side so pitifully that I cradled him in one hand and gently held him to my chest until he fell asleep.

It was two weeks later that I awoke to Jef pecking at my ear. The clock said 3 am, but Jef was wide awake.

'I did it,' he said quietly, his whole body trembling and his feathers drenched in sweat.

'Did you … did your dreams come true?'

'I caught the moment when time and sleep are one. Then I dreamt of myself flying back to my oasis and telling my family I was well. And I flew. I flew!'

'So … how are they?'

'They are well,' Jef told me happily. 'My niece has hatched her first brood and my father serves at the right wing of our new ruler.'

It didn't occur to me that Jef could have easily been lying, whether intentionally or not, for I instinctively trusted him despite the head-whirling impossibility of it all. The thought only struck me next morning. I was on my way to convincing myself that Jef had been mistaken when I went up to my room and found his cage still locked and unopened since I'd closed it the night before. For the rest of the day I was smiling so hard while thoughts crowded my head that people even wished me happy birthday.

But time only stops when we're asleep, and soon it felt like a lifetime ago that Jef had dreamt his way out of a locked cage and into the heart of the outback and his family. I grew without growing up, and boys started taking notice of me and I of them. I fell in love with Callum Briggs in French class and got slapped by Jodie Winters when I bumped into her and sent coffee all over her Gucci bag. By the time I was fifteen I was out of the house more often than I was in, my parents yelled at me for what seemed like the smallest things, and Jef and I barely got to talk. I'd stopped holding him to my chest when he got lonely, thinking about his family, because he was getting frail and because I couldn't bear the thought of any male, not even Jef, resting his head in that spot. But once in a while he'd wink at me and I'd hold him in my cupped palms while he nibbled my fingers and whistled his family's anthem, as if it had only been months, not years.

When Callum Briggs invited me to a rooftop party I had another screaming match with my parents where I could barely hear a word but knew exactly what they were saying.

'They think I'm too young and not responsible enough,' I muttered to Jef after I'd slammed my room door behind me. Slamming doors well was an art I'd had many opportunities to practise since I'd turned thirteen. It's a useful skill.

Jef didn't say anything and I interrupted my sulking to glance at him. He was staring out the window, one claw carving small tears in his newspaper as he'd do whenever he was down.

'Should I go?' I asked, not as bleating as before.

'You do what you do,' he murmured dryly, picking at a seed. 'Don't let an old bird like me run your life.'

This is when I took a closer look at him and saw with a shock that his wings were turning grey. He'd never told me his age but the years were there in his eyes and in the way his claws didn't grip so tight anymore.

'You've gotten old,' I said, brushing hard at my eyes, but determined to be mature. 'When did you get so old, Jef?' And I stroked his head in his cage even as my parents turned on each other in snide fury behind my door.

'It's all relative,' he whispered. But when he nibbled at my hand I could barely feel a pinch.

The rooftop was rented out by a posh club, an open-air loft of mercurial banisters and icy tiles sixteen floors up and overlooking the bay. The boys brought vodka cruisers while the girls brought lipstick and padded bras, and we pretended to be worldly and depraved as we swayed and sang self-consciously in the hot moonlight. There was no reason for the party other than the airs that affect fifteen-year-olds and make them grow older faster than they should. At some point I started kissing Callum Briggs. He put his hand on my breast, then unzipped his jeans in front of everyone.

'You know what to do,' he said, and his circle of mates laughed. Some of them followed suit with their own partners.

'No, I don't,' I said, suddenly afraid of what was happening.

He pushed me so hard that I fell to my knees, which was of course where he wanted me.

'Suck it,' he ordered, loud and confident with the vodka in him, and when he pulled it out red and straining in my face I was so shocked I scrambled away. He didn't look so beautiful anymore.

'It's too small, Cal,' one of his mates sniggered, his own already in Jodie Matthews' mouth.

'Fuck off,', Callum snarled and stumbled towards me as I tried to crawl away. 'And fuck you, too!' I hit the railing just before he hit me. Then the hand that had been so tentative just minutes ago, slapped me in the chest.

'Fucking suck it!' he yelled. He raised his bottle and I cried out because it looked like it was about to come crashing down on my face. Then, dimly, I heard the beating of wings, soft and vicious below the music. A second later Callum was flung back to slash across the concrete of the rooftop, hit by a blur of brown and gold. Jodie Matthews pulled her mouth back and screamed, while the guy who had laughed before was frantically trying to zip himself up and get away. I didn't want to look behind me, but I did. The wings could have easily enveloped the whole roof, while the yellow beak curved cruelly, fixed in a perpetual sneer. Only the eyes were familiar and the way they twinkled in the lights.

'You are filth,' said the eagle, and Callum must have been one of those who can hear the birds because he whimpered and curled up into a limp ball.

'Please don't kill me!' he cried.

'Please just fuck off,' retorted the eagle dryly before I was gripped by talons as cold as glass and pulled up into the air. My breath was whipped away by the wind and the height and the sheer velocity of it all.

The claws released me and I felt the dew of the front lawn tingle on my skin. I lay there on the grass for a second, too exhausted to move, then turned to my side and picked up Jef where he had fallen.

'Thank you,' I said to him, stroking the wings that were once again so small and old. 'Thank you, Mr Jef.'

'Get some rest, my lady,' he whispered. 'I won't run away.' His eyes sank shut and I felt him drift away. I didn't cry; it wouldn't have befitted him.

'Sweet dreams,' I whispered back, hoping that there might still be something left of him to hear me, and I held him close in my cupped hands until the dawn came.

THE MAN IN GREY

Amelia Dale

It was early Wednesday morning. I raised my red eyes to the red sky, and decided to discover where dead people go. Main motive? The girl in the flat next to me, a Venus with a bad haircut, had been murdered. Of course I could find out who did it, but I have tracked down enough psychos in my time. The drawing up and out of suspects, ripping off mask after mask until every face I see looks rubber. Gathering evidence, photographing footprints in flower gardens, analysing dust lodged in wrinkles of dead witches' faces. And in the end, all you get is that twinge of anticlimax because it is the person you expected all along. I am sick of it all. If I can track down who killed her, why can't I discover where she has run off to?

Her neck had been broken; her eyes were left as still and glassy as a doll's. The words 'You can't beat the man in grey' had been scrawled on her left cheek. It wasn't her writing. A clue to her killer? Probably. A guide to the afterlife? Hell, no!

I have never believed much in incantations, but I figured to try to raise the Devil would be a good starting point for my investigations. I have had some trouble believing in a benevolent God, but with my memories, it takes no effort to believe in Satan. That night, alone in my grimy apartment, I did an Internet search.

Google guided me to hundreds upon hundreds of different conjuring tricks: how to call the Devil at Halloween, what to say while standing in a bucket of pig's blood, the exact nature of the contract to be signed at night-time crossroads ...

I found several incantations of a more suitable minimalist nature. I thought not all of them might work, so I faithfully performed seven. I said all the magic words and cursed everything that could ever be sweet or sacred. I cursed the sky, children, my mother, love, pizza, good music.

By half past midnight there wasn't so much as a bolt of lightning, but there was a rotten taste in my mouth, like week old meat.

I lit up the TV and a cigarette and tried to absorb myself into the garish glories of late-night television. But I was the weary tyres screeching against the bitumen beyond the window. I was the dirty paper, peeling like skin from the wall. A minute past one there was a knock at the door.

'Come in.'

'You have to say it three times.'

I did.

He was shaped like a human, a balding human with a dusty suit and the beginnings of a beard. He could have sat next to me on the bus and I wouldn't have raised an eyebrow. He walked with a bit of a limp, then perched himself on the sad sofa.

'How's things?' I said.

'Could be better. Yourself?'

'The same, or I wouldn't be speaking to you.'

He turned the sound off the TV. 'Do I know you?'

'Do you want a drink?'

'I'll have some green tea, if you have any.' When he opened his mouth a bit of blood trickled out, he wiped it away with his sleeve.

'Sorry, haven't got any tea.'

'You look like a coffee drinker,' he said, wrinkling up his nose. 'And you smell like a smoker. I can't stand smoke, and I have to deal with it all the time.'

'I wouldn't have thought you'd cared much for green tea.'

'My health is all I have left,' he said primly, again wiping blood away from his chin. 'And I don't have much left of that. Things. People. Have been very unfair. I've got the blame for everything that doesn't work. And the only people who try to please me disgust me.' He started coughing, and blood cascaded across the wall. The cleaning lady was going to think I had been slaughtering whales in my living room.

'Excuse me, my last meal went down the wrong way. Since you say you haven't got any tea, you may as well come straight to the point and tell me why I've been summoned.'

'Do you know anything,' I said, stiffening my upper lip and putting on my policeman's voice, 'about the whereabouts of a Diane Sturgiss?'

'What do you want to do with her? Arrest her?'

'That's none of your business. I just want to know where she is.'

'She's in the mortuary, fool.'

'No, she isn't.'

He smiles innocently up at me, through bloodstained teeth. 'Isn't she?'

I couldn't stand that slimy-with-blood smile. I blame the smile on what I did next. I am not a violent person. I have been in a few fights and things, but I don't go looking for them. Apart from his smile, there was no reason why I punched him. 'Call me sir. You be respectful. I'm a police officer. Don't contradict me, if you know what's good for you.'

'What's good for me?' he repeated, still grinning, but there was a thud, and my fist hit his jaw as surely as if it was made of flesh and bone. He stared at me with swollen yellow eyes, like the bodies of toads. It was the first time in our conversation I had the sense to feel afraid.

'Would you like to see Diane again? Would you like her restored to you?'

'It depends,' I began.

'No, it doesn't,' he snapped, rocking in his chair, cradling his jaw. He clapped his hands once. The world went black and rolled away.

I opened my eyes. I was in bed and there was no blood on the walls. What a mad dream.

'Conjuring Satan. What junk.' I rolled over in bed and almost knocked Diane Sturgiss out of it. White cheeks, still lips and hips, a little pink marble near the nose and blue round the eyes, that mole and the ghastly hairstyle ... What was she doing there? What was she doing here? Wasn't the woman dead? I tried to wake her up, I shook her, I punched her, I rapped the side of her cheek — was she even real? Dead real and I had killed her. Had I just killed her then? Or had she already been dead? I seemed to remember ... Had I killed her before? I tried and I tried but no matter what I did, I couldn't remember. The universe beyond this dim room and her stiff body had floated away like an unrealistic dream. My brain was hammering brick wall punches against grey throats, my memory had sighed itself away like her breath.

This was what comes from swinging a punch at the Devil, I told myself. Why didn't I pay attention to my own warning? 'You can't beat the man in grey'. I wrote this advice on her cold cheek, knowing I wouldn't be able to understand it the next time it reached me.

I wandered out of her apartment, outside, onto the street. I hoped here I might breathe more slowly and deeply. I prayed here the traffic fumes and vile morning wind might sieve the present from the past. But instead I felt a growing numbness and even my confusion slipped away. I could no longer remember what I had been puzzled about. I knew she was dead. I knew the time and the day of the week. It was early Wednesday morning. I raised my red eyes to the red sky, and decided to discover where dead people go. Main motive? The girl in the flat next to me, a Venus with a bad haircut, had been murdered. Of course I could find out who did it, but I have tracked down enough psychos in my time.

THE NEXT CHAPTER

Alison Gibson

They work using soft voices, unwilling to disturb the silence. The soft darkness of pre-dawn gives gentleness to their act of disloyalty, but can't disguise it. My bed is stripped of its nonagenarian quilt, a family heirloom unused to movement, much like me. I sit on the bare mattress and watch my life being triaged; which knick-knacks could be taken? Which had the most sentimental value? And which sentimentality could I do without? Some photos, of course, would be allowed, but not too many; no point living in the past after all. This wasn't the end; it was the next *stage*, the next *chapter* of my life about to begin. The motivational-speak of countless garish TV personalities saturates their actions, and I resent it. The blatant lies told to a child. Neatly taped-up boxes of belongings greet the morning sun with a scowl, disliking the movement as much as I do. But hey, it's *breakfast time*, how about some eggs? Just like *Dad* used to make, sunny side up with just a *dash* of chilli sauce. Do I look sunny side up to you? Give me double-sided burnt with enough chilli to disintegrate the tongue, and a dash of whisky for good measure. Damn right I mean it.

A removalist's van appears; daily hire for a life's worth of treasure. And trash. Trash and treasure to match perfectly every other life, because by this stage they're all the same, covered in dust and forgotten lies.

We'd discussed it before, they had reminded me. As if that made it better. The thoughts of a decade ago being quoted to excuse today's behaviour. I was being *unreasonable*, I *knew* their situation, *they* didn't like it any more than I did. The beginnings of a scorching day's sun peeled itself onto us through glass windows I'd been looking out of for a lifetime. Glass through which I'd seen endless parades of neighbours dancing their way into another phase of their life, with endless new cars, dogs, partners ... And now the endlessness ends, how strange. These walls have sheltered me from countless thunderstorms which shook themselves in from the ocean, from baking midday suns which created crispy skin in minutes, even from that snowfall in the seventies when children thought they'd been thrown into heaven and cars went skidding across the icy roads to the horror of nervous parents. There was the time the drunk driver, a boy of twenty, smashed into the front telegraph pole in the middle of the night, breaking his legs and most of his teeth, and leaving blood all over my footpath. The time the schoolgirls came knocking, selling chocolate cupcakes they'd made, but ran down the front steps too quickly and knocked them all into the garden, chocolate and young girls' tears mixing with the dirt and ants. The time a woman with a child appeared on my doorstep, tears flowing, asking for help as she'd just left her husband ... and I let her in, and gave her a cuppa and a kind ear, before I sent her on her way. This home had been a refuge after my two-hour commute to work, a place in which I would never have to expect the unexpected, where everything had its place, including me. But now it was just *too hard*, they said; 'they' being the generation for whom it was meant to be easy. What was too hard? The *worrying*; the endless worrying about what might have happened to me, what was *going* to happen to me. Lucky me, always the topic of conversation apparently, and always because they were in expectation of some Big Event. Never mind that what *was* happening to me was red wine and game shows, crispy roast pork with a spongy apple sauce, or kind sunlight on old bare skin with no audience. Oh, but the *worrying* ...

Breakfast dishes are scooped up as the consolations continue to flow: we'll come visit, you'll still *see* us Mum, and — worst of all — think of all the *friends* you'll make. I'm six years old in a neatly pressed tartan skirt, pink backpack swinging from my shoulders and teary eyes being told in earnest that I'll have fun at big school, that I'll make so many *friends*. And then trundled off to be left in a building larger than my imagination can handle, surrounded by kids infinitely more informed and confident than I. At least I could run in the sun then. Now I'm lucky if I get a stroll down the garden path without five hats being thrown at me.

The door of the van is opened and I sit in the front. Looks pass behind my back but I'm still an adult; I'll sit where I like. The van is driven carefully, there's fragile cargo after all. Fancy that, thinking of me as fragile. Me, the robust one with strong shoulders, long arms, firm thighs. Not that you could tell now. But I still *feel* strong. Christ, I'm starting to sound like them. The house slides off the edge of the mirror and conversation is forced onward as awkward tears trail down my cheeks.

The careful drive ends in a careful park under a well-kept tree with strategically-grown shade-giving branches. There will be no frolicking here, but at least the tears have stopped.

Whitewashed walls in pale green wrap around corridors of spongy carpet to protect those *fragile* knees, hips, eyes. Nurses with boisterous smiles for me, sympathy eyes for them, guide us between stone-cold living statues of wrinkles. To think this is how they see me. A private room; oh, Mum how *fortunate* is that? As if I should have expected a dormitory of octogenarian schoolgirls, giggling whispers through the night. One of them leads me away for a *nice* cuppa — as if machines are capable of brewing nice cuppas — while the other busily decorates with All The Reminders of Home. The quilt, the photos, the knick-knacks carefully arranged when we shuffle back in, while the sun sliding through a half-open window brings a scent of singed grass, and a heavy fly floats across the room towards the door. Big hopeful smiles from them, hopes so strong their foreheads strain to contain the aching lines. Promises of phone calls and urges to go meet friends. And then silence. The small bustling room becomes empty of everything but mismatched memories, and I sit, trying to piece it all back together again.

THE RADIO

Bronwyn Lacken

Macy shuffled about the kitchen, clattering dishes and preparing tea. The December sun poured through the western windows, heat wafting lazily and inexorably through the thin panes of glass. With the table set, she allowed herself a spell on one of the green vinyl chairs, half in a stupor with the heat.

The beauty of the dust particles struck her as they danced in the river of light, and she followed the torrent with a bemused stare to the patch of bleached wallpaper that the sun had made, standing out like a white gateway from the surrounding brown wood-grain pattern. The process of deterioration seemed to accelerate as she watched, the light blistering the square of paper into scabs and then seething down the wall to pool and bubble on the yellow linoleum, bringing a nauseating stench to her nostrils.

She awoke to the sound of the chicken spitting in the electric frying pan, the smell of her dream dissolving into that of burning fat riding the waves of sunlight through the kitchen to the table where she was sitting.

'Yer silly old bat, whad' ya go an' fall asleep fer?' she muttered, hoisting herself out of the chair, slippery with her salt, and removing the two large slabs of chicken from the pan. She turned the appliance off and stared with a kind of hopeless incomprehension at the fat encrusted in its corners, a mixture of black charring and crisp golden brown. 'Needs a good clean out, that does,' she said vaguely, before turning to scoop the carrots, peas and broccoli out of the saucepan that bubbled on the stove.

The food slopped gracelessly onto the old cracked dinner set, and Macy stumped her heavy frame over to the small, rectangular table — yellow linoleum like the floor ('that's co-ordination, that is,' Mick had told her when they were first married) — and carefully covered Mick's plate with a tea towel. Mick always wanted his tea 'fresh an' hot' when he got home, and usually complained to Macy that it wasn't. She got the meal ready too early, as he always told her, though she didn't know what else to do, fearing those days when the bus got in early and there would otherwise be no meal on the table. She still had scars from the last time that had happened. So she continued to cook at the same time week after week, and used the tea towel in a futile attempt to keep Mick's food fresh and hot as ordered, always thinking it might work better next time.

Spending most of her time alone, Macy had gotten into the habit of talking to herself to try to fill the hostile silences of the house. Mick had inherited it from his parents, and she knew that it disapproved of her. During the early days of her marriage, when Mick had gone off to work and left her bored and depressed in the house, she had spoken into its corners and spaces in the hope that it would become accepting, even friendly. Twenty years later, she no longer expected it. But she kept on speaking nonetheless. These daily monologues had become the means by which she spoke herself into reality, pushing away the walls of oblivion that were forever closing in on her.

Mick's presence was announced by his habitual curse as the front door jammed halfway open on the warped floorboard that he insisted only needing sanding, not replacing. He blamed it on Macy, since it was her job to maintain the home while he was out in the world doing the real work.

Mick always wore a heavy overcoat home on the bus, to cover the stench of the meat packing plant where he worked as he would a dirty secret. Possessed of a brutal love of butchery and a crippling, bowel-loosening fear of being unrespectable, Mick had found his niche in the world in carving up dead animals, a way to slaughter and still be counted a productive member of society. So zealous was he in the execution of his duties that he had risen up steadily through the blood-spattered ranks over the years and was now the plant supervisor.

This was good. Mick enjoyed being deferred to, and it gave him a glow of pride when he looked down on all the busy workers, knowing that the fate of every one of them rested in his hands, that he had only to say the word and this one would be fired, that one moved to another part of the plant, a third put on reduced hours. The feel of the power was unparalleled, yet Mick was not entirely satisfied. As a supervisor, he was not often required to deal with the carcasses directly, and this, in his mind, was a shame. There was a part of him that still desired to cut through flesh and bone, to feel the rich, sticky blood on his hands that would ignite the burst of euphoria in his brain, shooting through his nervous system and making every inch of skin quiver in ecstasy.

The house echoed crooningly as Mick stepped over the threshold and trod heavily up the hall, wearing his scent of blood proudly now that he was in his own domain. Macy hurriedly seated herself at the table, numb to the sickening stench after so many (how many? she couldn't remember) years of exposure. She greeted Mick, but he threw only a cursory nod in her direction as he daintily lowered his barrel-shape body into a sticky chair.

Blood, he surmised for one exultant moment; but no, it was only Macy's sweat, the familiar scent of fear and sex that was almost as sweet. It seduced him, enfolding him with the promise of comfort, and he felt his brain itching with the desire to hurt. Mick was a master of pain, and there were many more sophisticated weapons in his arsenal besides mere fists. The one he brought out nightly at dinnertime was amongst his favourites.

They sat for a moment, two dumpy grey-haired middle-aged figures suspended in the yellow room, and Macy could almost feel as though she were outside herself, watching this static vision of humanity, waiting for the small movement that she knew was coming to force the act onwards. It seemed late to her, the ritual movement, and a part of her wondered in a sudden panic if it wasn't coming. She would be trapped in this moment forever, with the sun beating into the side of her head and a trickle of sweat suspended halfway down her back.

Then the solid block of Mick's arm cut through the light, reaching out to the shelf above the table and switching on the small portable Radio crouching squat and black on the shelf, a half-seen menace that hovered on the edge of consciousness. It was a deliberate movement, the timing carefully calculated for maximum impact, and Macy crouched into herself like a solider hunkering down in a trench to escape incoming fire.

The gravelly voice of the Radio reached out to Mick and Macy, drawing them forward in time and out of suspension. The waking of the mechanical God was the sign that the meal was now permitted to begin, and Macy picked up her cutlery reluctantly, contemplating the food before her without appetite.

Mick listened half-heartedly to the political segment of the six o'clock news, growling now and then at the preponderance of bleeding-heart reporters who he believed were responsible for the moral decline of the country. Why were they always sympathising, he asked, with those who were not completely human — the blacks, the migrants, the refugees locked up in the desert — and ignoring the plight of those who made up the backbone of the nation?

As he finished off the greasy chicken and started on the limp vegetables, Mick's favourite segment of the Radio news began — the crime reports. This was the primary reason he turned the Radio on every evening, to have the pleasure of listening to account after account of the perversity of human nature, though he never would have admitted this, even to himself. He was merely staying informed. It was not his fault that the information was ugly.

The news started with the murders, fathers who had killed their children, wives and girlfriends who'd been beaten to death in their own homes, bodies found in alleyways in drug-related assassinations, moving on to the more gruesome and interesting suicides, accidental deaths, and finally the road tolls. The veggies lay forgotten as Mick sat entranced, the torrent of blood and misery providing him with sustenance far beyond that of ordinary food.

This flow of darkness seemed to dim the aureate kitchen, Macy thought, though she knew that the sun would not set for another two hours. After a moment she realised it was because there were tears collecting in her eyes and obscuring her vision, an ineffectual shield against the horror of the Radio's intelligence.

She was never prepared for this inundation of suffering that flooded the kitchen, though it happened every night.

Afterwards, the event always seemed to recede from her, pushed into a corner of her mind so that she could convince herself it wasn't as bad as she remembered. To admit that the harsh knowledge force-fed to her by the Radio was reality, would be to accept that there was no hope. For herself or the rest of the world.

Mick's eyes greedily drank in his wife's reaction, his euphoria building like the spark of lust. A part of him knew how perverted this was, but that only increased his guilty fascination, his almost physical longing to inflict wounds so subtle and delicate they would not even be detected. Not quite as satisfying as the long-ago days of meat carving, but close.

'Someone should do something about all them awful, awful things happening. Where're the police when all of this is goin' on?' Macy's agonised voice burst into the room almost against her will, drowning out the number of collisions on the interstate highway. It was useless, she knew, to protest, and exactly what Mick wanted, but she couldn't just sit in silence and let the Radio have its own way, filling her life with visions of darkness and despair.

His face lit with hard delight, Mick stared at Macy triumphantly. He loved it when she resisted, when she gave him an excuse to be brutal. Her words hung in the sun-drenched air like spider webs between them, binding them together, drawing her, sticky and struggling, into his world, the world of the Radio.

'How can the police be expected to maintain a proper force when the government won't give them the funding they need?' Mick's voice, usually harsh, was quiet, schooled into the cultured tones of the newsreaders on the Radio. The voice of knowledge and authority.

'The bloody government should give them more money, then,' yelled Macy in a high nasal shriek. 'Take some out of their own back pockets. I tell yer, that's where all our hard-earned taxes go, into their fat bank accounts. The money's not being used to protect people like it should be.'

Stupid woman, Mick thought with savage pleasure. She didn't understand anything about how the world worked, about the inevitability of corruption eating away at society from within. 'You think those politicians care?' he said. 'The ordinary people don't matter to them. As long as they keep getting their big salaries, they think everything's fine.'

'Well it's not right!'

'It's the world we live in,' said Mick ruthlessly, enjoying the way Macy flinched.

The Radio was still droning on, but Mick and Macy dwindled into silence as light and heat intensified in the kitchen, Macy too defeated to speak any more, and Mick already pleasantly glutted on misery. Outside, the sun was fighting its death, sinking slowly beneath the rim of the earth in lurid shades of red. At Mick's order, Macy rose from the table and made two cups of tea, her rounded shoulders relaxing a fraction as Mick's fingers reached out and finally switched off the Radio, silencing its dreadful voice.

What the Radio said every night was always mixed up in Macy's mind with the world 'out there', the harsh and complex realities which lay menacingly in wait just beyond the front gate of the dowdy house, just past the strip of neglected lawn. There was a cowardly relief in her that she never had to go out there like Mick did, that she could stay inside and be protected.

Over the tea, weak because it was made from used tea bags (Mick did not believe in waste), Macy thought she recalled that long ago, when she was young, the world hadn't been like that, full of violence and death. The world had seemed good back then, but it couldn't be like that now, for the Radio said otherwise. A familiar self-loathing settled on Macy as she thought about how easily Mick and the Radio had lured her into arguing with them. She knew that Mick enjoyed tormenting her, and she hated herself for giving him the satisfaction every night. And she didn't even know why she kept on bothering, since it was so clear that the Radio was right.

But after a while, even Macy's humiliation began to fade, her mind wiped blank by the detergent as she cleaned the dishes. Forgetting, forgetting so that she could keep on going, another hour, another day, another year.

Perhaps, she decided, the news on the Radio would not be as bad tomorrow night.

Later, when sultry darkness lay over the city, Mick and Macy listened to Mozart and Verdi on the Radio. Mick liked a bit of culture. They went to bed early and lay wakefully side-by-side, ignoring each other's presence. Macy knew that there were other women, smelt their perfume and their youth on Mick sometimes, but the knowledge didn't affect her in any way. Whatever Mick did out there in the world wasn't relevant to Macy's existence, to her universe bordered by the four walls of the house.

The next day, after Mick left for work, Macy wandered wearily from room to room tackling her domestic duties. The heat was shimmering outside, marooning her in a sea of tar and concrete. Taking a bag of rubbish out to the bin, she found herself trapped, mesmerised by the horizon seductively dipping and weaving at the end of the street. She felt that if she could only move her eyes fast enough she would be able to see the heat in physical manifestation, a form of glowing orange fire stalking the black roads, withering all those hapless enough to cross its path.

When the pain in her eyes became powerful enough to bring her out of the trance, she returned to the grudging shelter of the house. She felt it chastising her for making a spectacle of herself to the curious eyes on the street. Mick, it seemed to remind her, was respectable and decent. He did not approve of unseemly exhibitions. Such things had the potential to bring down the standards of the country.

In the cocoon of yellow light that evening, the rusty red-brown of the chops contrasting offensively with the brilliant buttercup tabletop, the Radio poured forth a tirade against teenage pregnancy. The meat tasted of blood in Macy's mouth, though perhaps it had only been permeated with Mick's putrid stench. She swallowed with effort, almost gagging, feeling pain in her head and anguish in her heart, the mounting twin pressures that always preceded her outbursts, and knew that another of her doomed protests was about to begin.

She looked at Mick, but the angle of the sun on the side of his face made him a confused jumble of shining skin and craggy darkness. The Radio, sheltered on its perch above the window, was a black rectangular hole. Macy let the river of words wash over her, deliberately trying to avoid fathoming their meaning. She didn't want this to happen again. The same scene played out in endless repetition, so that she no longer knew whether she was living in yesterday or tomorrow, or whether they were all the same moment suspended in golden liquid light.

Glancing up at the Radio, Macy saw a strange flicker for a moment, whether in her own vision or the object itself she couldn't be sure. This had never happened before, a slight glitch in the seamless flow of one indistinguishable day to the next. She felt her chest expand as the realisation came to her that variation was still possible, and the merest glimmerings of power began to stir within her. The Radio is hiding something, she thought daringly, squinting through the air and trying to see more clearly. This too was different; she had never dared to question the Radio before, and in response the Radio seemed to blend into its own shadow, a solid, immovable bulk. Its voice became louder, rasping against the inside of Macy's skull. She couldn't shut out the words any longer. Understanding came in spite of her attempts to stop it, and she could feel herself spiraling again into the pain, borne along by its uncontrollable current.

'It's — it's the parents.' The words were torn from Macy by the power of the Radio. 'If people're goin' to have kids they need to be responsible; keep an eye on 'em. Stop 'em from havin' kids when they're no more'n kids themselves.'

'Yes, it's certainly to do with a lack of discipline,' Mick drawled, deliberately skewing the meaning of Macy's statement. 'But then, the parents who let their daughters get pregnant at such a young age are always utter morons, and that's why it happens. It's a never-ending cycle. The government should just sterilise the lot of them, stop them wasting the country's resources. That's the only way they'll ever learn.'

Mick turned his face towards the Radio, full sunlight illuminating his features. Macy didn't hear the rest of what he said, thrown out of her habitual stupor by his burning eyes, his thin lips twisted upwards in a mirthless grin. Shocked into a moment of clarity, Macy saw the sham of her life laid bare in the sunlight.

She focused on the babbling Radio with a hatred so intense she frightened herself. She knew this moment would never come again, a window of opportunity. She hung for a moment, disembodied, with light pouring through her, and then she reached through the air, lifting the Radio from its shelf and throwing it hard against the bleached patch of wallpaper on the opposite side of the room. The Gateway was opened and the voice of the Radio screamed as it drowned in the wholesome whiteness of oblivion. Shards of black casing fell through yellow air to solid yellow floor, electrical guts spewing across the linoleum.

A profound silence ruled, punctuated only by the trilling of cicadas outside in the garden. Macy noisily expelled a breath, breaking the tableau, and turned her head slowly towards the Radio's shelf, brushing over her husband's shocked wide eyes.

On the shelf, previously concealed by the Radio, there was a cheap plastic photo frame containing the picture of a girl with unruly blond hair and a lop-sided grin. Macy's hand shot out and grabbed the frame, Mick's fingers, too slow, brushing against hers as he tried to stop her.

Cradling the photograph against her, Macy stared at it in wonderment. The past was something she rarely thought about any more, or the future, her entire life concentrated only on enduring moment after moment. But this photograph was like raw power in her hands. It made her remember, reconnected her to a self she'd thought long vanquished by Mick and the Radio. It was summer. Macy was eighteen, laughing from beneath a floppy hat, wisps of hair escaping and curling around her face. She was wearing a knee-length cotton dress, the light fabric rippling in an invisible wind while a frozen ocean crashed on the shore behind her.

It had been before Mick, she remembered, before the hypnotism of the Radio, and as Macy held the depth and breadth of herself preserved on a glossy sliver of paper, she knew she could escape now. The Radio was in possession of her no longer; she had won herself back from it, and she would not let it capture her again.

Raising her eyes from the photograph, Macy looked steadily at Mick. 'I'm leaving,' she said firmly. 'Yer can't keep me here no more. Not now I've found meself again.'

'You won't survive out there.' Mick's voice was contemptuous, but Macy could hear the undercurrent of fear rippling through it. She had destroyed Mick's talisman and discovered her own, breaking her bonds, breaking his power, and she knew he was no longer certain of his control.

'Yes, I will,' she said, unconsciously speaking the way Mick did when he imitated the Radio. 'This photograph is everything I used to be. All the things I thought I couldn't be any more. When this was taken, I was confident, happy, I didn't need you. I didn't need to believe the things you say about the world. I thought I'd forgotten, but it's all still here in the photograph. As long as I have this, I'll be protected.' She brandished the photograph like a weapon, and then Macy rose from the table and turned her back on Mick, walking up the dim narrow hall to the front door without bothering to look back.

Mick wanted to kill her, more than anything, at that moment. There was a heavy lamp near his hand, and he could imagine picking it up and smashing it down on her arrogant body, her skull crumpling in on itself in satisfying defeat. Yet it was Macy's arrogance that caused him to hesitate. She had broken his rules, destroyed his Radio; what else might she prove herself capable of if he gave her the chance? It might only lead to further humiliation, to further erosion of Mick's already precarious grasp on what should have unquestioningly been his reality. What little was left had to be preserved if he was to ever have any hope of repairing the damage done to his realm, so he stayed where he was, hands clenched into fists, and only his frustrated scream of rage followed Macy up the hall.

Macy stepped out of the stuffy house into the cool twilit evening. Already Mick was receding from her mind, a demon whose power had been rendered impotent, forgettable. A breeze wafted gently down the street, caressing her skin and expelling the lingering taint of blood from her hair. With the photograph held safely in her hand, Macy lifted her head, threw back her shoulders, and smiled.

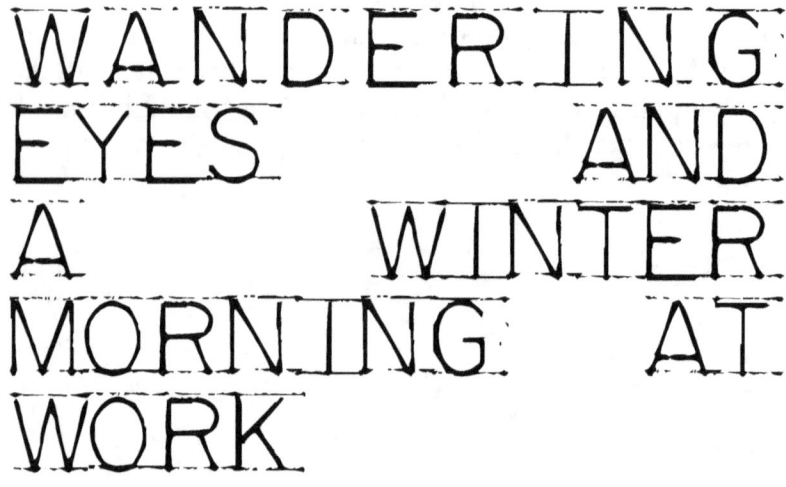

WANDERING EYES AND A WINTER MORNING AT WORK

Cipi Morgan

At work: My eyes wandered and found you there
Wandered all around that shadowy new face
Wandered all around the world of your hair
As you sat and your tongue found the taste

Of black coffee and toast — buttery and sweet
As the happy purse of your lips showed
For seven hours the two of you talked by the street
In this dim cafe buried under bright snow.

My elbow grew numb on the cold wooden bench
At my counter with work-sweaty hair
I watched your painted nails scrunch and clench
The cloth of the pretty window-table you shared.

Now he bends his head back and he laughs and he snorts
Your flesh sighs 'Love me, love me again!'
And you bent your head back with a laugh and I thought
Love *me* seven hours — or ten.

All his sparkle and canny and decadent jest
Were his own and he shared them with none
And your wildcat mad hunger, your mind which is best
Growled softly and meekly and glum

At last you strolled out from the coffee and heat,
From the delicious, dim view of snow
Freckles of ice flakes fell blue on pink cheeks
He said: 'I'm sorry I have to go ...'

And I watched from my counter, polishing brass
As he left you in his white after-chill
And you looked at me through the misted café glass
For the first time, breathless, hungry and still.

WARMER WINTERS

Elisabeth Murray

In winter, Sandy's memory was thick and rich as treacle. Perhaps it was the long train ride, the antiquity and quiet of her grandparents' property, the hours between breakfast and lunch and dinner spent adding or shedding layers of clothing, trying to reconcile the body to the frost and the shaky sunlight.

Was it the cold or the country? The time or the place? Who could separate them anyway? To Sandy, winter *was* her grandparents' house and she had never been home in the winter holidays for as long as she could remember. The thought frightened her.

Her memories the rest of the year were pale and spindly, too brief and dull to realise they were floating past in her mind, searching in the bathroom cabinet for pink pills, raised voices in the next bedroom, frozen dinners. But winter memories were different. They were hot as butter cake straight from the oven and bright as a painted rainbow. Prickling started behind her eyes or her stomach leapt, like the feelings of the past had leapt through the tunnel of time, just as strong as the moment of conception. It was times like these she felt she *was* someone. A classic Alice or Dorothy. Sometimes the flashes would be so electric she felt she'd stolen them from a film or a book or a picture. She couldn't tack them onto any sort of timeline, perfectly to scale, of how she imagined her life thus far. But she couldn't place them into anything she'd watched or read or seen, either.

It was on just such a winter moment on the farm fence that Sandy was overpowered by just such a memory. She felt the rasp of her woollen red sweater sleeve against her teeth; she was three years old, with dark curls and dark eyelashes that sat against her fat white cheeks. There were stacks of boxes, and a sea of photographs covered the living room carpet. Granma leaned over for a box and Sandy, sitting on the fence, breathed in the shampoo-cake-farm perfume of her hair. Sandy grabbed her grandmother's hair and laughed; Granma laughed too. She tugged her hair out of Sandy's grasp and gave her a shoebox that they hadn't opened. Sandy watched her dark curls plunge into the box and felt the cool shininess of photographs like water on her skin. She felt the dust overpower her nose. On the fence, she almost sneezed with the pitch.

'Oi there!'

Sandy's fingers scrabbled at the fence but it was too late — she fell on her knees and the heels of her palms hit the gravel. The rush of tears threatened her eyes and her throat, but she caught a glimpse of a boy, and she knew what hell she'd pay if she was seen to be a sook.

'What'd you do that for, Humpty?'

Sandy glared at him. In the silence that ensued she noticed his dust-blonde hair, denim jacket and brown shorts dusty with dirt.

'Your knee's bleeding,' he said, pointing. 'Aren't you gonna start crying?'

Sandy sat down against the fence and examined the split in her pants. Blood was dripping through and her knee looked like a burst volcano. Her palms were stinging and white with ripped skin. Thinking about what her Granma would say when she saw she'd torn her pants made her hurt even more.

'She's gonna start crying,' the boy said, addressing an invisible crowd standing around them in the road. He shoved his hands in his pockets.

'No,' said Sandy, picking herself up. 'That's okay, my Gran'll be able to put a patch on them in no time. Granpa's stuff's got leather patches all over the place. It'll be right.'

'Granpa? You staying at the farm there? That's why I haven't seen you round?'

'Well yeah,' Sandy said. She drew her knee up to her chest to examine it as she stood against the fence. 'I'm staying for my holidays. I always do.' She laid the back of her hand against her knee to feel the heat.

The boy frowned at her. 'Stop starin' at your knee. All you girls are always whingeing about blood and scratches. It's just a torn-up knee. It'll be a scab and then it'll go. Just let it alone, will ya?'

'I'm not whingeing,' Sandy retorted, letting her leg drop to the ground. 'I like looking at it. It's a real mess. Bet you haven't had one like that before.'

'Me?' the boy scoffed. 'I've had bloody thousands worse than that. One a mine wouldn't stop bleeding for a week.'

Sandy glared at him and looped her fingers through the wire fence.

The boy twisted his bottom lip with his fingers and turned away.

'How old are you, anyhow?' he asked.

'Eight,' Sandy said.

'I'm nine,' said the boy, with renewed fervour. He stood in front of her, hands in pockets. 'My name's Dakin. Tom Dakin.'

Sandy laughed. 'I was gonna say, that's a funny name. When you said Dakin. Tom, though, that's not so bad. You sounded like my Dad though. "My name's Dakin"!' She said it quietly to herself, and laughed again.

Tom looked at her crossly. 'Well, I gotta go. So go on laughing at my name.'

Sandy's face fell. 'Sorry, Tom, I didn't mean to —' But he had already turned away. She ran and caught his shoulder.

'What?'

'I wasn't laughing at your name, stupid. It was how you said it. But I just said it sounded like my Dad. You don't know my Dad. If you did, you'd want to sound like him.'

'Why? What's so hot about your Dad?'

'Oh, he wears a suit and he goes to work every day at the same time and comes home on the train and sometimes it's dark.'

'What's so hot about wearing a suit? I wore one to my auntie's wedding.'

'Well he works in the city. Bet you've never been to the city.'

'Oh. I guess I haven't.'

Tom turned away, twisting his bottom lip.

'Well that's okay. Maybe one day you'll work in the city and ... and I'll marry you.'

Tom looked at her suddenly. 'No you won't!'

'Even if I cooked bacon and muffins for breakfast and roast for tea and washed everything so it smelt nice on the clothesline and went to ladies' lunches in town?'

'What, is that what your mum does?'

Sandy looked through the fence towards her grandparents' house. 'Yeah. Of course that's what she does. Doesn't your mum?'

Tom shrugged. 'I guess. But she gets scraps for the pigs and milks cows and cleans the chicken coop and —' He took a breath. 'And all that as well.'

Sandy shook her head. 'My mum wears a white dress and high heels. You can't do that stuff in clothes like that.'

'Well I'm gonna own a farm when I'm old,' Tom said. 'So if you wanna wear junk like that I'm never gonna marry you.'

Sandy looked at the ground and thought. 'Oh well. I s'pose you'll give in when you see how glamorous I look.'

Tom rolled his eyes and folded his arms. 'It's teatime,' he said. 'I'll see you round.'

He turned and started running back down the brown road.

'Wait!' Sandy yelled.

He stopped a few metres away. 'What now?'

'It's not dinnertime yet. You're an old liar.'

'It is. Look at the sky.'

'You don't have a watch.'

'I know. So look at the sky. Bloody hell, are you always this dumb?'

'Look at the sky?'

'Look at where the sun is.'

Sandy stared at the sky. It was blue and soft with strips of clouds. By the time she looked down again Tom was gone.

Sandy strode across the farm and took her sandals off so she could feel the dry grass on her feet. She thought maybe it wouldn't be so bad living here when she was grown up and married. It might have been her favourite place in the world.

By the time she got to the door her toes were frozen blue and Granma snatched her inside, chiding under her breath.

'I've a good mind to send you to bed without pud.'

Sandy smiled, wrapped in her grandmother's flaccid arms, feeling like she was on a black and white sitcom and she was wearing a pinafore and was going to eat pudding in front of the fire — something like spotted dick or junket.

'But I'm not going to do that, because it's apple pie and I made the ice cream this morning.'

Sandy laughed because she could taste the warm and the cold and the sweet and the dough and the slippery and the gold and the white inside her mouth.

'And because I love you, my darling.' Granma knelt down and hugged her and their heads rested together and Sandy breathed in the shampoo-cake-farm perfume of her hair. It belted a memory into her mind like an advertisement. Again she was three, and dark-haired, and overwhelmed by dust. In the winter, memories were not only created but replayed and relived because this was the place that housed them.

Granpa came in with wood splinters on his cardigan and said, 'Wood's stoked in the fire for tonight, Eleanor.'

He knelt in front of Sandy and unbuttoned her blue coat. He hung it over a dining chair and rubbed her nose with his rough brown hands.

'You need a balaclava, Miss Sandy,' he said. 'Your nose is red-raw.'

Sandy laughed. She sat in the dining chair that was hers for the winter. The blue tablecloth was spotted with crumbs. Sandy looked at the salt and pepper shakers that were much, much older than she was. She looked at the tomato sauce and butter and apple cider that was foggy with cold. They were as much a part of winter dinners as the hot food. Sandy hated the bareness of the wooden table back home. It seemed wide as the ocean.

Sandy watched Granma at the stove squashing potatoes with butter and salt. She listened to Granpa in the living room starting the fire. She could smell meat and vegetables and winter.

After dinner they ate apple pie in front of the fire. Granpa sat in his armchair and Sandy in Granma's lap with her legs and arms tangled. Granma was telling her a story about a little girl she took care of a long time ago. 'What was the girl's name, Granma?'

Granma's breath caught and she looked at Sandy. 'Your mother, darling. I'm always telling you about your mother when she was the dearest little girl. You *are* silly.'

'Hey, no I'm not. Because you're always telling me about you and your sisters when you were small.'

'Oh, I am,' said Granma, and kissed her cheek. 'But they're different stories. Your mother had a lovely dress with coloured flowers that she wore for years and years until I convinced her she'd outgrown it. I bought her the loveliest dresses from town and made her so many as well because I was a wonderful seamstress, you know.'

'Yes. And it was because she was the only little girl and she had five brothers and you couldn't make them dresses.'

Granma smiled and said, 'Yes. She was my only little girl.'

Sandy looked over at Granpa and thought he was asleep but then he sat up and she saw he was listening.

'Well, my sweetheart,' said Granma. 'It's time for bed.'

Sandy was going to protest and ask for more stories about that little girl Granma had taken care of, but the fire had made her so sleepy she could only close her eyes and let Granma lead her into the bedroom. In a moment she was under the covers and Granma was murmuring that there was another blanket at the end of the bed to pull up if she was cold. And if she was scared or sad she could come into their bed. Granma was kissing Sandy and pulling the blankets up to her chin and Sandy felt warm and safe, then the lamp went out. Only pictures of winter went quickly through her head as she fell into the place before sleep. There was Tom, and the dust road and lamb chops and hot and cold sugar and Granma's doughy breath and the little girl in the psychedelic dress.

When Sandy woke she couldn't remember her dreams and she smiled because they always unsettled her. The light was cold and bright through the curtains and looked as if it might just shatter against the walls. Sandy got up and put on her slippers. She couldn't imagine staying in bed all day, every day. Once she'd had the flu so bad she had to lie in her room from when she woke up until night-time. Her legs got heavy and itchy and her head felt stupid and clogged. She couldn't imagine being so sick you never wanted to get out of bed.

Sandy padded into the kitchen. Granma was in her yellow dressing-gown praying. Sandy stood in the doorway and watched because it made her feel safe to see her grandmother's neck bent and her white hair covering her face and her whole body silent and still.

When Granma noticed her there she scolded her for being sneaky. While Sandy ate sausages and drank orange juice, Granma brushed her hair. The orange juice was thick and lumpy and made Sandy full.

After breakfast Sandy got dressed in her overalls. She clipped them up at the front and pulled on her red woollen jumper because she knew Granma would get cross if she tried to go out with a thin shirt and overalls. She pulled on two pairs of socks.

In the kitchen, a song about summertime and a rich daddy and a good-looking ma and nothing-gonna-harm-you came out of the radio. It made Sandy stop in the doorway. She watched Granma scrubbing the frypan. The window was open, the daisy curtains fluttered and cold wind blew over Granma's hair but she didn't shiver. When the song finished she noticed Sandy.

'Go out and get the eggs please, Sandy. I want to make a lemon cake and then you can have a slice for morning tea.'

The corners of her mouth crinkled like birthday present cellophane as she smiled. Her hair blew all over her face, but as she turned back to the sink it blew off her face, the same way as the curtains.

Sandy ran out through the hallway and through the front door as she hooked the egg basket over her arm. The air hit her hard and cold at first but after a moment it was fine. The chicken coop was warm and musty and probably smelt bad, Sandy supposed, but all she could think of was last winter when she was littler and Granma had to help her pick up the chooks and not break the eggs; how she sat back on her ankles with her knees in the muck counting the eggs in the basket, and she'd seen something silver that looked odd against the straw and the manure. When Granma saw it she coughed and was so surprised she dropped the chook and the egg. Sandy smelled dusty feathers as it flurried. Granma looked at the bracelet like it was a cut out heart. She said it was Sandy's mother's and clasped it on Sandy's wrist then went back to see how the chook was. Right now she could feel the warmth of the bracelet like something that had been buried and was hot with age and secrets.

The bracelet was thin and plain and had a piece of straw stuck in one of the links but Sandy felt proud because it must have been old. When she went home she showed her mother and she remembered it and kissed Sandy's palm but it didn't make her laugh.

Now Sandy sat in the straw under a chook's perch. Because of the dust and muck and chicken smell she could almost taste the memory of finding the bracelet. The memory of showing her mother was vaguer. She tried to call it up, make it crystallise, but it was as bleary as if she was looking through the eyes of a newborn pup.

Then something dripped onto her hand like warm sap and she jumped.

'Oh, damn it!' Sandy stood up and jabbed the basket at the chook. It made her feel better to swear. The hen flew onto another perch and squawked at Sandy like an irritable old lady. Sandy scraped her hand against the wall. She heard footsteps in the straw.

It was Tom. Sandy put the basket on the ground and linked her hands behind her back.

'How'd you get in?' she said.

'I climbed the fence,' he said. 'Have you got all the eggs?'

'Not all.'

'I'll help. I never get to collect eggs.'

In silence they walked around the barn and put their hands under hens for eggs. They felt hot satiny feathers and scratchy straw. To Sandy it felt like the warm silence at night in Granma's bed when she was little and scared of something she couldn't see. It felt like a big black bear over her bed when she was alone in the spare room. It made her cold. Granma told her it was her mum's bedroom when she was a little girl and that's why the curtains were still pink and there were Golden Books stocked in the cupboard that would tumble out like hastily-hidden evidence. But it didn't make Sandy feel warmer or safer. In Granma and Granpa's room there was a canopy that kept everything out. Then the silence made her feel full and contented as though she'd eaten Christmas pudding and Granma waited until she fell asleep.

That's how it was now in the barn. When they were finished they had more eggs than could fit in the basket, so Tom had to carry them in his arms. It made a laugh rise from Sandy's stomach to see it, but she didn't let it out of her mouth because she didn't want to upset the quiet. In the kitchen Granma was kneading dough. She looked strong and bad-tempered.

Sandy and Tom put the eggs away and Sandy was afraid of asking if she could go out and play, but Granma saw them and smiled like nothing could make her happier than to see them standing there.

'Well, Tom Dakin, isn't it?'

'Yes, ma'am, it is.'

'Well, you're looking fine. How's your mother and father?'

'They're fine too, ma'am.'

'I'm glad to hear it. Are you going out to play, Sandy?'

'Yes, Granma.'

'Well, you stay where you're supposed to, darling, and come home when you're hungry, and there'll be lemon cake.'

Tom chased Sandy out the front door and Granma went back to kneading her dough, no longer looking so cross.

Sandy and Tom jumped over the fence and landed on the brown road. They could still see Tom's footprints because no cars had come by.

Sandy was tired from running all the way across the yard and the wool of her jumper was prickly on her neck. She threw it off and felt cold from the air but hot from running. It was like drinking freezing coke then eating a meat pie that burnt your throat on the way down. It got so you couldn't tell the difference between the hot and cold.

'You look so bloody stupid,' said Tom.

'I'm tired,' said Sandy. She sat down with her back against the fence.

Tom fell down next to her. They didn't speak to each other. They listened to their breathing. It slowed down at the same time.

'Do you reckon your Granma would care if I came to eat the lemon cake with you?'

'No, probably not.'

'I like lemon cake. 'Specially when it gets heated up and it's a cold day.' His shoulders went up and his lips went inside his mouth like he was tasting it right now. 'Because my mum isn't so much of a cook, you know?'

'Really?' said Sandy.

Tom shook his head. 'It's kind of bad, because she's a mother and my mates have mums who bake stuff for the summer fair and everything. And they wear flowery aprons.' He shrugged and added, 'Stupid anyway.'

Sandy nodded. She sighed. 'Well, my mum doesn't wear flowery aprons. And I guess she's not so much of a cook either.'

Tom stared at her. 'You're kidding! After all you said about her being a wife that cooks like a whiz and ... and all the rest.'

'She doesn't cook too much,' Sandy said, twisting a rock into the dirt. 'Some days she's crook and she stays at home and she used to be in hospital.'

'That's too bad,' said Tom. 'What's she crook with?'

'Just off colour. Like out of sorts, my Dad says.'

'So why'd she go to hospital?'

Sandy hammered the rock further in with her fist. 'So they could shock her out of it.'

'Like when you got the hiccups and someone tries to scare it outta you?' said Tom. 'That doesn't never work.'

'Oh, I guess,' said Sandy. She wanted to get up and stamp on the rock. 'But my Dad says don't worry.'

She looked at her dirty hands and rubbed them on her overalls.

She shrugged. 'I know lots about wives anyway. Did you know, boys and girls hold hands?'

Tom jumped up like he'd been bitten. At the same time tyres crunched on the road and a silver car came up so close to them Sandy felt like she'd never seen a car before. It was as though she was on a safari close up behind an elephant.

Sandy leapt up next to Tom and said, 'That's my Dad!'

Tom had his mouth open. Sandy couldn't see the driver because the windows were so dark, but she knew it was him. The window rolled down and he leant out to kiss her.

'Hello, love.'

Sandy kept smiling. She looked back at Tom standing against the fence. 'Look, see, Tom, that's my Dad, who I was telling you about.'

'G'day, Tom,' Sandy's Dad said.

He was always nice to Sandy's friends. She felt proud when she saw Tom watching them, hands in his pockets. She was so happy to see her Dad, looking so out of place in the bare brown landscape. He was wearing his Sunday polo shirt, light blue. Sandy only thought now that it must be Sunday. In the winter holidays there was nothing unpleasant to remind her of a routine. There may as well have been no such thing as days of the week.

'Well, get in and I'll drive back to the house. There's some things I have to talk to Granma and Granpa about.'

Sandy opened the back door. 'Come on, Tom.'

Tom shuffled his feet in the dirt and shrugged.

'Sands, maybe we'll just go up first and talk —' Sandy's Dad began, but when Sandy looked over at him he just said, 'In you get, Tom.'

When Sandy felt the cold slipperiness of the beige car seats and breathed in the sharp mixture of air freshener and aftershave, a sudden anxiety invaded.

'Why are you here Dad?'

He grinned into the rear-view mirror. His eyes were green like hers, but his teeth were straight and white against his pink lips, while hers were crooked.

'Well, that's a way to treat your father.'

He stopped behind Granpa's truck and said as he turned off the car, 'It's just something small, love. Don't be such a worrywart.'

Sandy's Dad held her hand as they walked up to the door and asked Tom questions about his family and his holidays and did he play for the footy team. He didn't want to walk into the house without knocking but Sandy led him into the kitchen and went around calling for Granma.

She was out the back in the laundry, bent over a tub of soapy water, sleeves pushed up to her elbows. Sandy stood in the door and breathed in the lemony soap with the cold air settling on her back. Then she was little again, helping Granma scrub big faded flowery dresses, her hands warm and creamy with soap, and somehow the front of Sandy's red dress and her curls damp too. All around her was that warm lemony soapy smell and under her bare feet the linoleum was peeling like the thick spotted skin of a half-pared potato. There was full laughter everywhere and Granma was hugging her. When Sandy came out of the memory she felt disoriented, like waking from a dream trying to unravel what's reality and what's not, because the pitch of the lemony soap was still so strong, folded into the feeling of the tight hug.

'What's wrong, darling?'

Granma was standing in front of Sandy, her hands still coated in soap and some stray suds along her hairline.

'Nothing. Guess who's here?'

She dragged her grandmother up the back porch and into the kitchen.

'Oh my goodness.' Granma stopped in the doorway then rushed over to her son-in-law. 'What's happened?'

She pulled down her sleeves and smoothed down her hair, but the soap was still there. 'How are you? How's Dana?'

Sandy's father stepped back and smoothed his shirt.

'Sandy, love, you go and play with Tom for a moment while I talk to Grandma.'

Sandy looked at him. His eyes were still bright, but Granma's eyes were flicking from him to the children. Now she looked like the one who wanted the hug.

'Love, haven't I told you not to worry?' Her father pushed her out of the kitchen and shut the door. A moment later, he had done the same to Tom with a sigh like the one he made when he had just walked in the front door and the phone rang.

Sandy and Tom stood staring at the door. Then she led him into her bedroom at the back of the house. The bed was made and the curtains opened.

'Let's climb out the window and jump over the fence,' Sandy said.

She knew what was behind there: a lane tangled in a near canopy of shrubbery, weeds and thorns. It was dark, and if you sat down it felt like you were in a forest.

'Your father would get angry.'

'Then let's go to your house. You've never invited me all this time. You know, a gentleman wouldn't do that.'

'He'd get *angry*, Sandy.'

'Shut up, what do you know? My Dad doesn't get angry.'

She took a breath to tell him about a time that proved this, when her father entered and said, 'Where are your things, love?'

'Why Dad?'

'Your mum's feeling a bit under the weather,' he replied, opening drawers and taking out her folded clothes. 'Where's your —'

'Dad, she's always under the weather, though, you said —'

'Sandy, I *know*, but come on, I don't have time to argue about it, your grandmother — Where's your suitcase?'

Sandy climbed onto her bed and leaned over the end rail. She pulled it onto the bed and her father unzipped it and threw the clothes inside.

'Get the rest of your stuff together, Sandy. Now.'

'But Dad, why's mum under the weather?'

'Under the weather?' Granma appeared at the door, followed by Granpa. Her hands were on her hips. There was a lump in her cheek, like her tongue was trying to poke through and start sounding off, but she'd pursed her lips to keep it quiet. 'Under the weather, Brian?'

'Sandy, come on, love. We've got to go.'

'Yes, you do, Brian.' Granma strode into the room and took Sandy's jeans from the wardrobe. She took a pile of underwear out of the chest of drawers and stacked them inside the suitcase. She went over to the bed. She lifted the pillow and withdrew Sandy's folded pink pyjamas. As she put them inside the suitcase, she brushed Sandy's hand and Sandy had a sudden memory of warm skin on hers like that, soft pressure on her hand, while she was lying in bed, and the smell of soup.

The memory was technicolour and full, but finished before Sandy could make sense of it, and she was watching Granma on her hands and knees, retrieving a sock, a plastic doll and a book from under the bed. Granpa put Sandy's toiletry bag and hairbrush in the suitcase on the very top and zipped it shut. He looked very serious, but after a moment he looked down at Sandy and smiled.

Before she had smiled back, her father had pulled her to the front door, her suitcase swinging against his legs.

'Where's Tom?' Sandy stopped inside the door while her father marched out.

'I think he left, darling,' said Granma, holding the screen door open. 'He must have sneaked off home.'

Sandy looked out over the balding grass. 'He must have thought you were angry. He must have thought you were upset.'

Granma stood still. 'You'll see him next winter, darling.'

Sandy's Dad yelled for her as he loaded her suitcase into the boot.

'Goodbye, angel,' Granpa said. She stood on tiptoe to kiss him and his beard tickled her face.

'Goodbye, darling,' Granma said, bending down and wrapping her arms around Sandy. Her arms were tight and Sandy breathed in lemon soap and lemon cake and winter.

Sandy stepped onto the red dirt and breathed in the cold air like was storing it up. She bit her lip and the inside of her cheeks all at once against the thought of the hospital, pure white and hard with hard feelings, without care or sustenance, where all the memories got locked out.

THE END

Polina Madorsky

I want to tell you that the end of all stories, even if the writer forbears to mention it, is death.

This is a story about writing, and the goal of a writer is to make the invisible visible within the mind of the reader. In reality this is not possible, but in this world of fiction it must be. I understand that this may confuse or anger you, but you must succumb to the slow gentle handshake with sanity. The writer must join you in listening to the invisible and in turn, enjoys the handshake with your insanity.

Allow me to tell you a story. It is a story about a girl. Everybody knew what she was and who she was, but nobody, anywhere knew her name. Without a name does she exist? Things come into existence once they are named. However, this unaccounted girl cannot be lost if no one is looking for her. Even if they were, how can they call her if they don't know her name? Her story is not one that can be passed on, and yet it is.

She is no more than words crawling along a dry page — my invention.

I created this girl and she became a part of me. I do not know her, but she exists. I cannot name her, because I believe she already has a name and I cannot rename her. She visits this page and becomes the page itself. This is a page where her story could be written, but it never will. So she becomes a story that people tell and argue over which version is the 'real' one. However, she stays out of all their tale-telling as she is aware of the dangers in entering a story. In her mind's eye the story will close in around her and trap her.

I am writing the story of this girl, and yet she escapes it.

Am I the girl who is too wary of entering a story and, hence, tries to hide away within confusing rhetoric?

Or am I the man you saw this morning with an amusing Adam's apple and cranberry lips?

I am getting frustrated with writing this tale and it is only the beginning. Well, to you it is the beginning — I on the other hand, have read and re-read these lines too many times. I have trapped my character within this page, within these margins, within these words, but you, dear reader, are bringing external forces into these words and margins.

This story is coming to an end. I can't even disguise it. I could place many blank pages to trick you but you will notice I have not done this. As this story progressed I became increasingly aware of beginning this story and the problem of an end. Perhaps the very fault does not lie in my lack of knowing how to end. Rather the fault lies in the very nature of beginnings and endings. As one begins a story we constantly expect to reach the end

ACKNOWLEDGEMENTS

The Editors would like to thank the Department of Media and Communications and the School of Letters, Art and Media at the University of Sydney for their support in the publication of this anthology.

We would also like to personally acknowledge Craig Silvey for writing an amazing introduction, and Keith Stevenson for all his guidance and support.

Thanks to you all.

The Editors:

Jessica Angell	Danielle Joseph
Tim Armitage	Kathryn Knight
Kate Bateman	Kathrin Moosmang
Alexandra Bednarczuk	Katharina Muders
Ailin Bezzo	Helen Palmer
Kate Calhau	Karin Pfaff
Heidi Cassell	Lauren Robb
Tom Champion	Yeong Sassall
Annie Chiv	Bridget Slater
Susanne Gierds	Eduard Stoklosinski
Emel Gusic	Luke Telford
Laura Heard	Alex Vitlin
Lydia Jauncey	

www.ingramcontent.com/pod-product-compliance
Lightning Source LLC
Chambersburg PA
CBHW051512260626
47162CB00008B/2941